LANGUAGE AND LITERACY SERIES

Dorothy S. Strickland and Celia Genishi

EDITORS

The Complete Theory-to-Practice
Handbook of Adult Literacy:
Curriculum Design and Teaching Approaches

*Rena Soifer, Martha E. Irwin, Barbara M. Crumrine, Emo Honzaki,
Blair K. Simmons, and Deborah L. Young*

The Complete Theory-to-Practice

HANDBOOK OF ADULT LITERACY

Curriculum Design and Teaching Approaches

RENA SOIFER   MARTHA E. IRWIN

BARBARA M. CRUMRINE

EMO HONZAKI   BLAIR K. SIMMONS

DEBORAH L. YOUNG

TEACHERS
COLLEGE
PRESS

Teachers College, Columbia University
New York and London

Published by Teachers College Press, 1234 Amsterdam Avenue
New York, NY 10027

Back cover photo of authors, courtesy of Public Information, Eastern Michigan
University, Ypsilanti, MI 48197.

Library of Congress Cataloging-in-Publication Data

The Complete theory-to-practice handbook of adult literacy :
  curriculum design and teaching approaches / Rena Soifer . . .
  (et al.).
     p. 197 cm. — (Language and literacy series : v. 1)
  Includes bibliograhical references.
  ISBN 0-8077-3028-9 (alk. paper)
     1. Reading (Adult education)—Handbooks, manuals, etc. 2. Adult
education—Michigan—Handbooks, manuals, etc. 3. Adult education—
Michigan—Curricula. 4. Reading—Language experience approach.
I. Soifer, Rena. II. Title: Handbook of adult literacy.
III. Series: Language and literacy series (New York, N. Y.) ; v. 1.
LC5225.R4C66   1990
374'.9774—dc20   90-31682
                                                                  CIP

ISBN 0–8077–3028–9 (pbk.)

Printed on acid-free paper

Manufactured in the United States of America

97 96 95 94 93 92 91 90   8 7 6 5 4 3 2 1

Contents

Foreword

Over the past few years public interest has increasingly focused on the issue of the high rate of adult illiteracy in America. Although the statistics vary in accordance with various definitions, it is abundantly clear that the problem has reached major proportions, with well over 20 million individuals being incapable of reading at what are considered "adult" levels of functioning.

The issue itself is not new. Since before our nation's independence there has been an understanding that reading and writing abilities are necessary skills in a modernizing environment, while at the same time a great many people reach adulthood without having mastered them adequately. Accordingly, organized efforts to teach literacy skills to the adult unlettered date back to the early Colonial period. However, throughout the history of American education these efforts have been viewed as secondary to the main thrust of instruction: that directed at children and youth in schools.

Attending contemporary changes in the economy and in scientific and technological knowledge, the problem has now become even more acute. Skill levels that may have been adequate a generation ago no longer suffice. The essential definition of what constitutes "literacy" in the waning years of twentieth-century America has undergone significant change. If a fourth grade level equivalency was considered the necessary benchmark during the early years of the century, the standard has now been revised upward to at least a ninth or tenth grade level. Clearly, as the definition changes, so does the scope of the problem. Unfortunately, poor attainment in many of our nation's schools only serves to exacerbate matters. Not only are high schools experiencing inordinately high dropout rates, many of those who do graduate are proving unable to read, write, and calculate at the desired levels. Without engaging in the ongoing "numbers game" as to how many "new" functional illiterates are annually being added to the adult population, I will argue that any number should be unacceptable.

Due in large part to the heavy emphasis put on formal school-ing, the field of adult literacy education historically has been a sorely neglected area of concern. What concern *has* been evident has all too often expressed itself in various pronouncements, but rarely in the allocation of appropriate means with which to prop-erly research issues and develop instructional approaches and cur-ricula. As the severity of the rates of illiteracy becomes more widely appreciated, calls for action rapidly follow.

Unfortunately, however, practitioners find that the resources they have to lean upon are extremely thin. While there is a body of accumulated, experientially derived, know-how—and to a lesser extent, research-based knowledge—there is only a very slim liter-ature available to both students of the field and its practitioners.

The Complete Theory-to-Practice Handbook of Adult Literacy is a welcome addition to the literature. It provides as up-to-date a pre-sentation of the practical and applied aspects of the field as is cur-rently available. There is no doubt that it will prove to be a valu-able tool to those engaged in the continuing struggle to grapple with illiteracy—not on the "macro" level of definition and policy, but on the individual level of learners and their learning needs.

DAVID HARMAN, PRESIDENT
INSTITUTE FOR CORPORATE EDUCATION
NEW YORK CITY

Preface

The Complete Theory-to-Practice Handbook of Adult Literacy contains guidelines for teaching approaches and curriculum development based on recent research about adult learning and the reading and writing processes. This material is designed for teachers of adults in public school and community education programs, business and industrial settings, and correctional institutions, as well as for administrators and educational advisors of those programs.

Our major premise is that whole language teaching and learning principles provide a viable framework for effective adult literacy programs. Adult learners are actively involved in listening, speaking, reading, and writing about content significant to them; thus they acquire strategies that enable them to learn how to learn. Classes are organized and lessons developed around the needs and interests of adult learners rather than pre-packaged materials. Reading and writing are used as tools for learning and teaching, rather than looked upon as subjects to be taught. The focus is on people in the process of acquiring increased competence in the abilities they need to become lifelong learners.

We believe that literacy in the information age extends beyond reading, writing, and GED (General Educational Development) preparation. Continually changing technology is widespread in society. Adults must learn to use new equipment, adapt to unfamiliar operating systems, and prepare for continual developments and changes. They should become familiar with computers in situations that are built around their needs and interests and that involve them actively with language—listening, speaking, reading, and writing. Thus they acquire the means for gaining proficiency with computers and, more important, for adapting to changes in technology.

Our purpose for writing this book is to share our experiences in implementing a program based on a whole language framework. In Chapter 1, we explain the implications of "adult literacy" and describe the principles of "dynamic interaction" that we believe underlie a successful program. From the history of literacy movements in the United States, we identify the challenge for adult literacy programs and propose that a program built on learners' backgrounds, language, interests, and needs is an effective way of responding to that challenge. In the next four chapters, we, teachers directly involved in various areas of adult literacy programs, describe the curriculum planning and teaching activities that we have found successful. The chapters on reading and writing (Chapter 2), GED preparation (Chapter 3), and computer awareness (Chapter 4) each include an authenticated course organizational plan, illustrative lessons, and suggestions for materials. In Chapter 5, we provide a rationale for integrating technology into adult literacy programs and offer suggestions for software selection and computer activities in reading, writing, and GED subjects. Because the staff is vital to the implementation of the philosophy, Chapter 6 is devoted to selecting teachers and helping them become familiar with the principles and practices of an interactive theory of adult learning. Comfortable and accessible physical facilities are essential; these are described in Chapter 7, along with suggestions for recruitment, publicity, and recognition ceremonies. Assessment of adult learning is challenging because it is often equated with standardized tests that are neither appropriate for adults nor reflective of current knowledge about reading; alternative instruments and procedures are mentioned in several chapters, and an overall assessment plan is included in Chapter 7.

The authors are all involved in The Academy, a literacy project in which the goal is to increase adults' self-confidence and abilities for learning how to learn. The teaching and learning approaches of The Academy are based on a whole language framework. Whether reading, writing, studying for GED, or using technology, learners in The Academy engage in meaningful discussions about content pertinent to their lives and work experiences. Established at Eastern Michigan University in 1979, The Academy program focused initially on reading and writing. Over the years the program expanded to include instruction for GED and computer awareness, with each addition carefully planned to follow the principles of interactive learning in which the instructors and learners talk, think, read, write, compute, and learn together using topics based on learners' experiences.

One of the authors, Rena Soifer, established The Academy and continues to inspire and direct the program. The other authors have been involved for many years, some of them having started as volunteer tutors while in graduate school. The Academy model was used as the basis for an educational program established in a local Ford Motor Company plant in 1984 under the sponsorship of The UAW–Ford National Education, Development and Training Center, a leader in promoting workplace literacy. All of the authors have been involved with that project.

We wish to express our appreciation to the many adult learners with whom we have worked over the years who have helped us grow in our understanding of effective literacy programs. We have gained as much—or more—from them as they have from us, which only shows that collaborative learning is valid not only for learners but for teachers as well. A special word of thanks is extended to Gene Henderson for allowing us to print his poem, a work that has inspired us all.

Whenever six people collaborate, someone must coordinate their efforts and make the text flow more coherently. We are grateful to Martha Irwin for undertaking that responsibility. Without her enthusiasm, gentle prodding, writing flair, and endless "to do" lists, this book would not have made it to the publisher.

Finally, we would like to thank our patient editors at Teachers College Press, Sarah Biondello and Nina George, for their support, advice, and encouragement. We also appreciate the careful work of the copyeditor, Myra Cleary, and the efforts of the many other behind-the-scenes people involved in getting our book into print.

Acknowledgment

Although this book was written by six people, the visionary behind it is Rena Soifer, an enthusiastic, warm, dedicated, and insightful teacher. Her professional life has been devoted to supporting and encouraging literacy and the love of learning in everyone with whom she comes in contact—workers on the plant floor, single mothers, prisoners, immigrants who need help with the English language, office workers who want to go to college, and fathers, mothers, and grandparents who are striving to make the world a better place for children and grandchildren. Rena's philosophy of education is consistent with her interest in people, based on a sincere respect for each learner's abilities, background, experiences, thoughts, and language. She has the insights, the drive, and the persistence to put her philosophy into operation. She is a model, a mentor, and an inspiration to staff members and other educators.

On behalf of all the learners and colleagues she has influenced over the years, we wish to pay tribute to Rena Soifer for her contributions to the promotion of adult literacy.

BARBARA M. CRUMRINE
EMO HONZAKI
MARTHA E. IRWIN
BLAIR K. SIMMONS
DEBORAH L. YOUNG

≪ 1 ≫

A Dynamic, Interactive, Whole Language Framework

You, the reader, are an adult learner. We, the writers, are adult learners. All of us continue to expand our understanding of the world, in general, because we are interested in people, places, and events and because we want to keep up-to-date with developments and knowledge. We realize that by continuing to learn, we gain pleasure and self-satisfaction and feel more successful in our home, social, and work lives. We seek to learn more about adult education, in particular, because part of our lives is dedicated to facilitating the learning of other people. Learning is satisfying to us and we want to help others experience similar rewards. We know that lifelong learning is as necessary in our profession as it is for the people for whom we are providing services. In essence, adult learning applies to all adults.

This book, however, focuses not on the total population but on undereducated adults who are developing their abilities for lifelong learning. They may be people who want help with reading and writing, ranging from those who are just beginning to interact with print to those who wish to read and write with greater ease and comprehension. They may be people who desire to complete their GED examinations for their own sense of fulfillment as well as for becoming involved in other areas of study. They may be people who would like to learn to use a computer in order to approach technological tools of the information age with confidence.

Literacy does not simply mean acquiring or improving reading and writing skills, completing GED examinations, and being able to manipulate computer programs, however. These are merely the means to much more important goals, which are central to the planning of effective adult literacy programs: self-realization, awareness of the reality of change and the need for lifelong learning, and abilities for learning how to learn. A concept of adult literacy that takes these goals into account is described in the first part of this chapter.

In order to implement a literacy program that incorporates skills as means for reaching those goals, the backgrounds, interests, and desires of adults must serve as the foundation for learning. Because people vary greatly in their experiences, wants, and expectations, the literacy program must be adaptable to different learners and changing circumstances. A dynamic curriculum based on interactions among learners and teachers is essential. The second part of the chapter elaborates on the rationale for a dynamic, interactive framework and describes the range of interactions that is needed.

Many adults, both those who need help and those who wish to serve them, recognize the need for literacy programs. Nonetheless, despite the efforts of many dedicated professionals, the problem of adult literacy still exists. Why is this so? What are the underlying challenges to literacy efforts and how can adult educators respond to them? Perhaps part of the problem lies in the assumptions being made about adult literacy programs, as indicated in the third section of this chapter. Perhaps part of the solution lies in looking more closely at how adults learn and how curriculum can be adapted to their lives. A whole language framework, described in the fourth section, is proposed as a way of responding to the challenges. Principles for guiding a literacy program centered on learners conclude the chapter.

ADULT LITERACY

Adult literacy encompasses much more than basic reading and writing skills. Harman (1987) maintains that a definition of literacy that refers simply to abilities to read and write is inadequate in that it does not give a sense of the content or purposes of the reading and writing, nor does it indicate how these purposes and goals vary in relation to the individuals within unique societal groups. Hunter and Harman (1979) use the term "functional literacy" to reflect a broader perspective. Functional literacy is defined as

> the possession of skills *perceived as necessary by particular persons and groups* to fulfill their own self-determined objectives as fam-

ily and community members, citizens, consumers, job-holders, and members of social, religious, or other associations of their choosing. This includes the ability to obtain information they want and to use that information for their own and others' well-being; the ability to read and write adequately to satisfy the requirements *they set for themselves* as being important for their own lives; the ability to deal positively with demands made on them by society, and the ability to solve the problems they face in their daily lives. (pp. 7–8)

Literacy in this larger sense has important implications for educators involved in planning and implementing adult programs. Reading and writing taught with a focus on skills—recognizing words, paraphrasing printed text, identifying parts of speech, and writing complete sentences—do not relate directly to the purposes of learners. The goal of learners is not to recognize words, but to extend their knowledge of the world and their abilities to function more effectively in everyday life and work situations. Although skills such as recognizing words are means to that end, such skills need not be taught as entities apart from the adult's interests and goals, that is, as prerequisites for later application to real situations. Fortunately, reading and writing abilities can be attained in ways in which learners accomplish personal goals at the same time as they increase their competence with the skills and strategies. By engaging in a range of communication activities about a topic of interest, learners gain confidence in listening, speaking, and participating in groups as well as reading and writing.

To be literate in today's world, people must also feel comfortable using technology. They must be able to use various tools for recording, accessing, organizing, and disseminating information as well as be competent with mechanized equipment in the workplace. As Applebee, Langer, and Mullis (1987) point out,

> The technological and information systems available to individuals at both home and work have accentuated the differences in opportunities available to those who have well-developed literacy skills and those who do not. On the one hand, technology is reducing the literacy skills needed to complete routine tasks; on the other hand, the skills needed to develop and control these technologies are becoming increasingly complex. While the needs of the work force do not require that all individuals have advanced literacy skills, the lack of such skills can prevent them from attaining positions that they may desire. (pp. 6–7)

Indeed, technology increases the need for literacy skills. People will soon be using computers and communication networks as a matter of course, if they are not doing so already. Many workers must be able to use word processors, databases, spreadsheets, graphing programs, computer-aided design programs, and robotics. These are only some of the types of electronic equipment available now. Who knows what the technology will be like tomorrow? People must be willing and able to adapt to changes readily and independently so they can approach new versions or even completely new technologies with confidence. They must be alert and able to locate quickly and assess with a critical, evaluative mind the wealth of information that technology makes available to them (White, 1987).

The principles for learning to use computers are similar to those for operating other forms of electronic equipment such as communication networks and robotics. Therefore, an adult education program might well include a computer component to provide opportunities for learners to become aware of the functions and gain control of technology. Adults can learn the concepts and functions of computers by using them to accomplish meaningful tasks, rather than by learning about them in an abstract way, such as through programming or listening to explanations about their inner mechanisms. For some people, computer awareness courses will enable them to feel secure in using the equipment. For others, wisely chosen software programs and activities can be incorporated within reading, writing, and GED lessons to enhance learning in those areas while at the same time giving adults experiences with the uses of technology.

DYNAMIC INTERACTIONS

Some powerful principles underlying adult literacy are indicated by the phrase "dynamic interactions." The phrase has gained prominence recently as a result of advancing knowledge of the reading process. Reading is now defined as a process of constructing meaning through the interaction among the reader's background knowledge, the information suggested by the text, and the context of the reading situation (Anderson, Hiebert, Scott, & Wilkinson, 1985; Rumelhart, 1977; Wixson, Peters, Weber, & Roeber, 1987). Reading is an active process in which the reader connects information from the text to information in the mind. The connections are made by a reader in the act of fulfilling a purpose in a situation that is meaningful to him or her. In short, reading is dynamic and interactive, and the prior knowledge and purposes of the reader are significant elements of the process. Reading is an active process, not a product or series of skills to be learned. The result of reading is new insights and knowledge in the reader's mind, not simply answers to comprehension questions or paraphrasings of text.

Borrowing and building on the phrase "dynamic interactions," implications can be seen for all phases of an adult literacy program: reading, writing, GED, computer awareness, and other subjects. Dynamic interactions should occur among

1. learners, materials, and purposes
2. learners, other learners, and teachers
3. teachers, research, and practice
4. teachers and other teachers

Each of these interactions is elaborated on in the paragraphs that follow.

Learners, Materials, and Purposes

Learning in any subject is a dynamic process in which learners make connections between their background experiences, materials appropriate to their needs and interests, and real-life situations. Adults have a wealth of background experiences, which vary from one person to another, and they are faced with numerous situations to which they must respond. Packaged lessons, with a prescribed scope of content and sequence of presentation, do not and probably cannot respond to these varied backgrounds, purposes, and changing situations.

Learners, Other Learners, and Teachers

Teaching is a dynamic process in which learners and teachers engage in dialogues and learn by listening to and interacting with one another. They share their wealth of knowledge about the world, raise questions about facts and opinions presented, and become sensitive to factors and interpretations that give new meanings to familiar ideas. Interactions occur among the learners as well as between teacher and learners. Kazemek and Rigg (1985a) believe that the one-on-one tutoring approach should be questioned because it fails to take advantage of social learning opportunities. Furthermore it "confirms (or exacerbates) the tutor-as-Parent graciously donating time, effort and skills to the needy student-Child" rather than takes advantage of learning "with and from each other" (p. 26).

Teachers, Research, and Practice

Effective teaching and learning occur when adult education programs connect research and theory with practice. Knowledge about the adult learner and principles of adult literacy (Brookfield, 1986b; Knowles & Associates, 1984) support programs that recognize the wholeness of learners and respect their educational backgrounds and personal experiences. Programs based on such insights enable learners to become active participants in the learning process in a climate in which they assume a status of equality with peers and teachers. Connections between theory and practice are particularly important in the areas of reading and writing, which are the focus of many adult literacy programs. Insights about the interactive nature of the reading process (Pearson, 1984) and the writing process (Elbow, 1973; Murray, 1982; Zinsser, 1985) should form the basis for learning activities. Teachers must be aware of the theory and research and use it to support their instructional practices. Otherwise, traditional approaches are perpetuated, such as "bottom-up" reading and writing lessons where the focus is on sounds, words, rules, and skills as prerequisites to, rather than components of, the real thing.

Teachers and Other Teachers

Dynamic interactions should occur among the teachers in the program. Like learners, they too profit from collaborative efforts. Involvement with other teachers helps them gain new insights about adult literacy, become part of a supportive network of people who have similar interests and concerns, and develop curricula that take advantage of interrelationships among the subjects they and their colleagues are teaching. Not only do teachers need to share information about research concerning adult literacy, they need to interact as they coordinate efforts for publicity, recruitment, and retention and as they plan for interrelationships of learning activities such as using computers as tools in reading, writing, and GED lessons.

In this text, then, the phrase "adult literacy" is used to indicate a broader focus than the common interpretation of adult literacy. The concept of adult literacy as used here is based on the recognition that the adult occupies a central role in the process of learning and that dynamic interactions of many kinds are crucial.

CHALLENGES FOR ADULT LITERACY PROGRAMS

A survey of the history of adult literacy efforts over the years indicates that literacy attempts have been based on a restricted outlook and that a more encompassing view of adult literacy is needed (Hunter & Harman, 1979; Kazemek & Rigg, 1985a). Since the 1880s recurring outcries have swept across the country concerning the high rate of illiteracy among the adult population. Educators and the media have sounded warnings about possible consequences of widespread illiteracy in the United States. Solutions were attempted, but after a time interest subsided and little was accomplished. Kazemek and Rigg (1985a) call adult literacy "America's phoenix problem" in that the crisis is identified anew about every 12 years, but the "crusade burns out within a few years" and "about a decade later, from the ashes, the same crisis arises" (p. 1). They maintain that

> The problem of adult illiteracy in the United States exists and appears to be getting worse because of mistaken assumptions about the nature of literacy. These mistaken assumptions result in definitions of adult literacy which are arbitrary or abstract and which are unsupported by empirical research. Moreover, these assumptions have resulted throughout the decades and continue to result in a host of inappropriate teaching materials and strategies and the continual funding of misguided training programs for adults. (p. 18)

In their report, Kazemek and Rigg identify several myths about adult literacy that have led to effects such as: blaming the victim for not being able to read, designing programs on a simplistic view of literacy that fails to recognize that literacy varies with the materials and with the situation, having people who can read "give" skills to others (all-knowing teachers depositing skills in unknowing students' heads), presenting such unrealistic standards of literate people as to be discouraging to the learner who feels far removed from ever reaching those models, and trying to make literacy programs cost-effective by having too many diverse learners in a class or by using untrained people as tutors (pp. 18–26). The challenge is to make changes in adult literacy programs in order to break out of the cycle of attempts that fail because of questionable assumptions—only to be reinstated in a few years with the same assumptions and with subsequent repeated failure.

Six years before the Kazemek and Rigg report, Hunter and Harman (1979) called for a substantial effort at the national level to address the large problem of illiteracy in the United States and to identify and disseminate significant research about adult literacy. Their two-year nationwide study of adult education programs documented the scope of illiteracy and indicated that the quality of life in the entire society could be negatively affected if reasoned planning and funding were delayed. They made a plea for pluralistic, community-based programs and presented the rationale for taking a new look at program planning for adults. Their recommendations are based on a view that adults have potential and should be involved in and responsible for their own learning by participation in decision making about program purposes and design. Although a scattering of educators was stimulated to rethink existing practices, there was not a widespread response to the study, and instruction continued as usual within most adult education programs.

In the 1980s, a continuous stream of books, newspaper and magazine articles, and television documentaries about adult literacy appeared. The purpose of this nationwide publicity effort was twofold: to inform people about the extent of illiteracy and to stimulate them to become involved, either as learners or as volunteer tutors. In many cases, the urgency of the problem was stressed by linking illiteracy to the nation's economic well-being. The media efforts were bolstered by results of the National Assessment for Education Progress (NAEP) report (Kirsch & Jungeblut, 1986), which indicated that many young adults are unable to apply their math and reading skills to meet the demands of daily life. Indeed some authorities (Johnston, 1986; U.S. Department of Labor & U.S. Department of Education, 1988) responded to that report by suggesting that by the year 2000 the nation's work force would be unable to compete in the marketplace due to a lack of essential literacy skills.

But the money and effort for this latest reawakening were spent on advertising the extent of the problem and motivating people to get involved rather than on looking at alternatives to the adult literacy programs that had surfaced and resurfaced over the years without the hoped-for results. Although a few alternative approaches were portrayed in the media, the underlying implication was that quantity was a major part of the answer—more adult learners, taught by more untrained tutors, and undoubtedly with more use of traditional approaches.

One of the few books to appear that addressed programmatic issues was by Harman (1987). Again, as in the earlier Hunter and Harman (1979) study, a major recommendation was for community involvement, with assistance to provide "technical guidance in aspects of program design, curriculum and materials development and training" and with a focus on the processes involved rather than on "'packaged' curricula and instructional approaches" that would not allow "customizing programs to suit local conditions" (p. 102). Furthermore, since literacy is dynamic and learning is lifelong, programs should be permanent rather than "one-shot" efforts. In Harman's (1987) words, what is needed is

> ... an adult education effort with a changing curriculum that would become a permanent part of peoples' lives, available as an aid to the continued growth and development made necessary by constantly changing conditions and definitions of literacy. Such a system of education has become an imperative of our time: anything less cannot properly address the central literacy-related dilemmas society faces. (p. 104)

This challenge is recognized by industry leaders as well as by educators. General Motors Chairperson Roger Smith (1986), at a Private Industry Council meeting, warned that "if we do what we've always done, we'll get what we've always got." Smith was calling attention to the traditional basic adult instruction that is not meeting the needs of the potential worker or the workplace. Since the early 1980s industry has recognized that workers need retraining because of

1. the intense competition among industrialized nations in marketing their products
2. the increased use of technologically advanced equipment
3. changing job requirements

Workers are expected to be self-directed, flexible, and open to change. In addition, they must be problem solvers, decision makers, thoughtful questioners, critical thinkers, and participants in work teams. With such demands in the workplace, it is apparent that the focus must be on education for ongoing growth—learning how to learn.

A WHOLE LANGUAGE RESPONSE TO THE CHALLENGES

How do adults learn how to learn? How can teaching be a dynamic process? How does the learner become an active participant in learning? What kind of framework will allow flexibility for the learner and the teacher? How can the next phoenix arise from the ashes in a new and more lasting form?

While the problem of combatting adult illiteracy and promoting lifelong learning throughout the population cannot be solved easily, this handbook is an attempt to respond to some of the challenges. A whole language framework for adult literacy instruction is advocated. The phrase "whole language" summarizes the basic principle that language is the medium for the learning and teaching of all content and is meaningful only when it is *whole*. Language is the vehicle through which learners' needs and interests are expressed, learners and teachers are engaged in collaborative efforts, learners' background knowledge is accessed and activated, and information from printed and computerized sources is gleaned. Reading, listening, speaking, and writing—the tools for learning—are incorporated in lessons in all subjects. All of these language areas are interrelated and interdependent; they nurture each other and are mutually strengthened as each becomes stronger.

The "whole" in whole language is significant. Whole language means just that—using whole language, not bits and pieces. Whole words, whole sentences, whole paragraphs, and whole texts will optimize the interaction among the learner, the content, and the context (situation and purpose). Furthermore, the social aspect of language learning is recognized. Language is the natural vehicle for social exchange. In a program based on a whole language framework, learners first engage in talking about what they know about the topic. They realize that they do know a lot. They listen to and learn from one another. They raise questions and make hypotheses about the subject. They read to add information or reconstruct meaning in their own minds. They write to organize and interpret the information gained, construct new meanings, and apply understandings to their own lives. They read their writings to peers who listen, talk, react, and extend the ideas. The content must be authentic language, "everyday, useful, relevant functional language," especially in the beginning, and then gradually "move through a full range of written language—in all its variety" as the learner achieves competence and success (Goodman, 1986).

Small group instruction is strongly recommended (although, as indicated in Chapter 2, in some cases individual tutoring may be necessary, at least in the beginning). Small group arrangements are ideal for practicing and expanding language and for taking advantage of the knowledge of the others in the group. Not only does the group setting promote learning of language skills and content, it serves as a simulation for the quality circles, self-directed work groups, and collaborative work teams that are becoming standard procedures in many workplaces today. Many adults soon begin to transfer some of the group procedures to their work and family situations (Soifer, Young, & Irwin, 1989).

Whole language learning in a group setting demands an environment that is physically conducive to interactions and psychologically safe for making comments and sharing ideas. Furniture arrangements in which group members can face one another as they speak are important. The psychological climate is even more crucial. Groups are settings for building self-esteem, having purposeful interactions with peers, and learning in an atmosphere where people can differ and question, yet value and respect, one another. Working in groups is like looking in a mirror to see more clearly who we are and what we believe. The opportunity is available to use the group as a sounding board for an idea. Learning with others is ideal for authentic language learning, since from birth one uses real language in social settings with significant others facing real-life situations.

The teacher is a facilitator (Brookfield, 1986b) rather than an authority figure who knows and attempts to impart knowledge in the sequence and manner that he or she deems appropriate. Because the typical view of teachers is that of authority figures, the adult facilitator must be very sensitive to learners, making sure they feel free to ask questions and agree or disagree with one another and the teacher. The facilitator serves as a model—listening, showing interest, and accepting contributions from all—so the learners realize that others care about their ideas and that it is safe to make mistakes. The manner in which the facilitator listens, respects ideas, and encourages comments and questions sets the stage for the group members to become involved in learning as a collaborative effort. The term "facilitator" indeed indicates a different view than "teacher." Because it is a more common term, "teacher" will be used throughout this book, but the broader meaning of facilitator is assumed. The word "learner" is used rather than "student" to indicate that the adult is a collaborative and active participant in learning, rather than a recipient of lessons.

Since learning is the learner's responsibility, so too is the assessment of progress. The teacher aids the learner in setting goals, and both are involved in ongoing evaluation of progress toward those goals. With a focus on becoming an independent learner, evaluation must take into account progress toward assuming responsibility for one's own learning. The teacher provides the framework for the learner to take command of maintaining attendance records, completing assignments, editing and revising materials, helping peers, and selecting materials for personal reading. Pre- and post-testing results can be used as guideposts for ongoing informal evaluation. A variety of formal and informal measures might be used to obtain a complete picture of the learner as a reader. Formal reading tests, however, must be chosen carefully and used with caution, since educational measurement does not yet reflect research on the reading process (Valencia & Pearson, 1987).

The concepts of whole language, dynamic interactions, and student involvement may sound ideal but vague at this point. What do they look like in action? Applications of the principles to reading and writing are described in Chapter 2, to GED in Chapter 3, and to computer awareness classes in Chapter 4. As you read these chapters, keep in mind that whole language provides only a framework, not a prescriptive method, as it must if instruction is to be dynamic, interactive, and adapted by teachers and learners in varying local situations to many types of content. The suggested lessons in the chapters are only models—examples of how the principles might be implemented. The model provides consistency; adaptation to specific learners provides individualization. Recommendations for course length and class meeting times are offered within the chapters, but they too must be adapted to local situations. The recommendations are for situations in which teachers have some voice in determining the length and time for offering sessions. In settings where such matters are predetermined, as in community education programs, the teacher must of course work within the constraints.

Chapter 5 deals with the use of computers as tools within reading and writing improvement classes and within the GED subjects; suggestions are offered for incorporating computers as an integral part of adult education programs. Because adult literacy is based on a premise that teachers are facilitators and because teaching is often seen more as telling than facilitating, staff selection and development are important; Chapter 6 considers these concerns about personnel. Matters relating to the overall structure of an adult literacy program are presented in Chapter 7, including such things as physical facilities, recruitment and publicity procedures, recognition and awards for learner achievements, and assessment techniques.

GUIDING PRINCIPLES

A whole language framework in a dynamic interactive environment encompasses fundamental beliefs about learners, teachers, learning, and teaching:

1. Education empowers people. It gives people the means to make rational decisions for themselves about their lives and their educational endeavors.
2. Learners are whole people whose wholeness must be consciously recognized. Their educational backgrounds, their personal experiences, their work situations, and particularly their language and cultural backgrounds must be respected.
3. Success is imperative from the beginning. Experiencing immediate success helps adults view themselves as learners and creates positive self-concepts.
4. Adults are responsible for their own learning. Strategies that foster self-determination are essential.
5. The teacher serves as a facilitator who plans and guides instruction. The learner is viewed as an equal, working with the teacher toward shared goals. Often teacher and learners are learning together.
6. Teachers must model and provide guided practice with specific strategies in all content areas. Teachers must be carefully selected for their understanding of adult learners, for their familiarity with teaching and learning strategies, and for their knowledge of specific content.

7. The environment has a strong influence on the quality of teaching and learning. Both the physical and the psychological climate are important.
8. Learners and teachers need to be aware of progress. Assessment is an ongoing process with both instructor and student involved. The celebration of successes is the focus of evaluation.

A simple caveat—there are no quick, easy answers for helping the vast numbers of adults who have limited or inadequate basic skills to become successful learners. But perhaps a new cycle can be set in motion—a positive cycle wherein successful adult learners realize personal benefits, inspire their peers, and serve as models of readers, writers, and learners for their children and grandchildren. In the eloquent words of one grandfather, a 30-year auto worker,

> There is a school in this plant you should attend,
>> Your social life and education you could mend.
> I know what's in your heart, you are no different from me,
>> It can't be the money because this school is free.
> Don't be backward, ashamed or afraid,
>> Just think of this school as studying a trade.
> If you think someone will laugh, rag you or even grin,
>> Ask them along—see if they are really your friend.
> It's so nice to read and, what you read, understand,
>> Makes you feel like you can communicate with any man.
> When you are sitting at home all alone,
>> You can write a letter and not use the phone.
> The teachers we have are so nice and sweet,
>> Just talking to them is really a treat.
> It won't take long—a few hours you can spend,
>> But it's impossible to finish if you never begin.

GENE HENDERSON

≪ 2 ≫

Reading and Writing Improvement

Helping adults improve their reading and writing ability is not a difficult process; however, the teaching must be stimulating, challenging, and nonthreatening in order to be effective. Most adults who are nonreaders or poor readers have negative feelings about reading and writing, previous schooling, and themselves. They must be helped to overcome these feelings and improve their self-esteem. It is imperative that adult educators emphasize the capabilities of the learners, thus helping them recognize and build on their strengths. Learning will occur when people realize they can learn and that it is exciting, satisfying, and rewarding to do so.

A whole language framework is used as the basis for determining lesson content and devising teaching/learning strategies that build on the strengths of adult learners and respond to their affective needs. Characteristics and components of lessons based on a whole language framework are overviewed in the first section of this chapter. Next, suggestions are offered for organizing a reading and writing improvement course to include those components. The bulk of the chapter is devoted to an elaboration of the four components of a typical session: uninterrupted sustained silent reading, activities based on learners' writings, guided reading and discussion, and writing. Finally, an illustrative lesson with a focus on comprehension is presented.

The lesson components are applicable to adults with all levels of abilities and can be used in group or individual settings. Suggestions are appropriate for all areas of adult education, although the primary emphasis here is the teaching of reading and writing. No artificial distinctions are made between reading and writing; they are approached as language processes and are further supported by other language processes—listening and speaking.

CHARACTERISTICS OF LESSONS

The phrase "whole language" refers to an outlook, a philosophy, a belief system—not a method of teaching. Evolving from a synthesis of insights from applied linguistics, psycholinguistics, sociolinguistics, anthropology, epistemology, and cognitive psychology (Goodman, Smith, Meredith, & Goodman, 1987), whole language emphasizes the relationships between language development and social interaction. Listening and oral language develop in meaningful situations where the emphasis is on understanding and communicating with others. Reading and writing are ways of extending one's interactions with people near and far in distance and time.

Meaningful lessons are centered on purposeful interaction and communication rather than on the study of language elements. Effective reading and writing activities involve constructing and imparting messages, ideas, and feelings. They do not center on studying the elements of language (letters, sounds, parts of speech) as prerequisites to the real processes of reading and writing. Those elements are important, of course, but are learned as a result of the need to use them in the process of sharing thoughts and ideas rather than in preparation for future applications to reading and writing.

In essence, learners need to read and write messages. In their lessons they need to use whole texts (articles, stories, books) with which they can interact to construct meanings that build on the prior knowledge they have about topics. They need opportunities to interact with other readers and realize that meanings are relative to individuals and not dictated by the printed marks on a page. They need opportunities to write messages, as a means both of communicating with others and of organizing and gaining clearer understandings of their knowledge. Furthermore, by writing their own thoughts they come to realize that printed materials are written by others like them and that authors include and exclude ideas in light of their purposes for writing and the audiences being addressed.

COMPONENTS OF READING AND WRITING LESSONS

An organizational framework for adult reading and writing improvement lessons can be designed around four components:

1. uninterrupted sustained silent reading
2. guided reading and discussion
3. writing
4. practice activities

Uninterrupted Sustained Silent Reading

Opportunity for uninterrupted sustained silent reading is a rarity in the busy lives of people today. Learners need time during which they read whole texts they have selected about topics important to them. A time for reading is important, for it is clear that one of the best ways to learn to read is by reading (Smith, 1973). If each lesson has a time when everyone, including the teacher, reads silently, learners realize that practice is essential. Furthermore, the learners sense the teacher's belief that they are capable of choosing materials and reading them.

Guided Reading and Discussion

In addition to independent reading, adult learners benefit from guided reading and discussion during which strategies are modeled and practiced. By participating in group discussions before, during, and after reading, learners expand their knowledge. As they listen to comments and reactions from other readers, they realize that different interpretations of text materials are possible.

Guided reading activities should reinforce the concept that reading is the dynamic process of interacting with the text and that readers are responsible for constructing meaning by using the background knowledge they possess to assimilate new insights. Strategies must be demonstrated and readers must be led to use them so that they take control of selecting and using the techniques that will serve them in the interactive, constructive process. Traditionally, strategies to improve comprehension have been sorely neglected, if not ignored, at all levels of reading instruction. Comprehension is often assessed by asking questions to make sure learners understand, but this is testing rather than teaching. Answering questions posed by the teacher does not help readers acquire independent strategies for gaining meaning from and interacting with printed materials. An even greater concern is that many adults know how to read in the traditional sense, that is, they can decode, but they have minimal strategies for understanding text. "What they don't know is how to evaluate what they read, how to see it in terms of who they are and other things they know, how to test in the pulses the real assumptions beneath the ostensible ones" (Coles, 1983, p. 119). The challenge to the teacher is to model and guide the reading and related discussions so learners acquire and apply independent strategies.

Writing

Writing activities have merit for both promoting writing ability and enhancing growth in reading. Building on the connections between writing and reading is appropriate for learners who are at the very beginning stages as well as for those who are more advanced. People learn to read through writing because their own experiences and language form a solid base of known information from which the only "new" element is making connections with the printed form of that language. One of the many values of writing activities is that comprehension is inherent when materials are created by the learner.

Language experience activities can be incorporated easily within a whole language framework. Language experience simply means recalling experiences, forming ideas, and developing thoughts on a topic, and then expressing them first orally and next in writing. This process is aided by the use of thought-provoking topics, articles, and stories, which trigger discussion and thinking, which, in turn, lead to writing. Adults who perceive themselves as nonreaders and nonwriters (or who are perceived as such by the teacher) can succeed with writing activities based on their experiences. Because the focus is on assets rather than on deficits, the learner realizes he or she is a capable person, not a failure. By building on the connections between writing and reading, that is, by using learners' writings as the basis for learning to read, individualization is achieved more readily than by trying to match learners with a packaged program in the hope that the materials will meet their needs and, what's more, satisfy their interests and capabilities.

Some teachers wonder how adults with few skills can engage in writing activities. Initially the teacher might record the thoughts of a person with very limited abilities. Gradually the learner will progress to writing his or her own materials. Some who are truly nonwriters and nonreaders may progress more quickly and feel more comfortable learning individually with a teacher or tutor. The teacher should be sensitive to the feelings and needs of each person and arrange for the best possible learning situation for the individual. The concept of the self-fulfilling prophecy must be kept in mind, however. If the teacher believes that the adult has such a low skill level that he or she cannot participate in a group setting, that expectation reinforces the person's already firmly planted notions about himself or herself as incapable of learning.

But simply having learners write is not enough. Regardless of their abilities, learners should be guided through the phases of the writing process: generating and rehearsing ideas, drafting, revising for content, and editing and proofreading for mechanics (Calkins, 1986; Emig, 1983; Fulwiler, 1987; Goldberg, 1986; Graves, 1984; Hansen, 1987; Sommers & McQuade, 1989; Zinsser, 1985, 1988). While the phases of the writing process overlap and are not necessarily sequential, each contributes in a special way to reading and writing development. Discussion on a relevant topic precedes the writing; this activates background knowledge and helps the learner see relationships and gain new insights about the subject. A draft is written, at which time thoughts are clarified and elaborated. During revision, the writer is guided to attend to organization, coherence, point of view, summarization, and further clarification of thoughts. In editing the text the writer is helped to understand the importance of conventions related to paragraphing, punctuating, capitalization, grammar, and spelling.

Learners' written materials provide opportunities for reading. Furthermore, writers gain an awareness of the ways in which authors develop and present thoughts, and thus their ability to understand texts written by others is enhanced (Goodman, 1986; McNeil, 1987).

Practice Activities

During reading and writing activities, particular needs of individual learners will emerge that may require additional practice. As they write and then read their work, they practice various ways of recognizing words: by sight, by using context clues, by becoming aware of structural elements (roots, prefixes, suffixes), and by realizing the sound–symbol relationships (phonics). However, more practice is often needed for automaticity, but taking time to do so during the reading and writing phases distracts from attention to comprehension and communication. The further development of skills is fostered by a knowledgeable teacher who makes sure that additional practice is provided on vocabulary, spelling, and word recognition. Practice materials are derived from the activities of the guided reading and writing phases of the lesson. Adults are not faced with grown-up versions of workbook-type lessons with which they apparently did not succeed as children—and which are based on an assumption that a defensible scope and sequence of skills can be identified, an assumption that is not verified by research (Downing, 1982; Samuels, 1976).

In addition to activities with vocabulary and word recognition, comprehension strategies must be modeled by the teacher and practiced by the learners. To become independent, readers must be aware of their own learning processes and use strategies that enable them to reach their potential. If their learning is to become self-directed, they must be aware of how learning occurs, that is, they need to understand *why* strategies are used and *how* they can apply those strategies on their own. In practice sessions, readers can be helped to understand the rationale for the strategies they have observed and experienced during the guided reading phase of the lesson.

Specific practice activities must be purposeful and brief. Above all, purposeful reading and writing provide unequalled opportunities for practice.

CLASS ORGANIZATION

Language is the medium for communication and for learning. To make the most use of that medium in all of its forms, interaction among learners and teachers is essential. Learning in a group setting makes it possible for the individual to contribute to the learning of others as well as to benefit from the knowledge of others. More important, in a small group setting an attitude of camaraderie develops—a respect for fellow classmates and an appreciation for the thoughts and feelings of others—which serves to enhance educational progress. In such a setting, true feelings of empathy are displayed; class members are sensitive to each other's feelings regarding educational background, reading and writing ability, and embarrassment or reluctance to perform in class. An encouraging, supportive environment helps learners to overcome their inhibitions about expressing themselves, both verbally and in writing.

Teachers who create this type of environment are rewarded

when they observe people developing a positive self-image after being in a group for just a short time. It is equally satisfying to see this improved self-image reflected in the kind, quality, and amount of reading and writing produced. Even more exciting is to observe the changes in attitude and ability as perceived by the learners themselves.

A small group means just that—small. Ideally a class should have a maximum of 10 learners. With no more than 10, each learner can be an active participant in class discussions and can receive individual attention from the teacher, both of which help the person realize a sense of self-worth. If circumstances warrant it, a group might have as few as two; for example, a group of two readers might engage in collaborative learning as well as provide psychological support for one another. However, grouping by ability is not necessary and is not recommended. Learners with differing levels of ability may be placed in the same class. No matter what their reading or writing strengths, all can participate in discussions. Since the materials are written by each learner, the vocabulary and the background information are inherently appropriate.

Whether working with one or ten, the teacher must plan carefully. Consideration must be given to overall organizational matters—the duration of the course, the length of class sessions, and record keeping—as well as to the plan of each lesson.

A reading and writing improvement course might be scheduled for a duration of eight or ten weeks, with ninety-minute, twice-weekly sessions. This period of time is appealing to adults, many of whom have extremely demanding schedules. Others may have a history of failure in educational experiences and thus are hesitant to enroll for several months or for an indeterminate time. Adults who might be unwilling to commit themselves to a lengthy educational program or who are unable to follow through with a seemingly unending commitment are receptive to a class of this length. They see a short-term goal with an end in sight—a stepping stone rather than an interminable bridge to cross. If they attend all sessions during an eight- or ten-week period they will receive twenty-four or thirty hours of instruction and practice. During this time, they are able to overcome inhibitions they may have regarding attending this type of class, to set and achieve short-term objectives, and to establish some long-term goals. Even for those who begin as nonreaders and who know that a few weeks will not be enough for them to learn to read, it is important to get started and have a short-term goal in sight—to reach the first stepping stone. Taking one day at a time is good advice; taking one eight- or ten-week reading and writing improvement session at a time makes equal sense.

Many adults experience success in this endeavor for the first time in their lives. They realize anew the importance of learning and become excited about and sometimes even addicted to it. Because of this, many will choose to continue and will enroll in another session. In future classes, strategies and methods for improving reading and writing ability will be reinforced and expanded upon, using the same approach but different materials. Generally, the need for this reinforcement through continuing classes is recognized by most adults and proves to be an incentive for them to enroll for the next session.

Learners benefit by involvement in keeping their own records; this helps them build self-confidence as they develop an awareness of their accomplishments. One way to organize record keeping is to have them develop personal portfolios of materials collected in file folders. During the first class, each person might be given one manila file folder for records and one colored folder for writings. Stapled into the manila record folder are various forms, such as a chart for attendance and writings (Figure 2.1), a page on which to list titles of books read (Figure 2.2), a graph for recording periodic assessments of vocabulary and spelling (Figure 2.3), and a place in which to note beginning and changing goals (Figure 2.4). Copies of the learner's writings will be fastened in the colored folder, which in turn will be placed in the manila folder. The folder should be labeled and stored in a filing cabinet in the classroom, with the appropriate drawer clearly marked and accessible to learners. Each person should also have a 3″ × 5″ box, with his or her name on it, containing alphabet dividers for filing vocabulary cards (which will be described on the following pages).

LESSON FORMAT

A typical lesson might be organized around the four interrelated components presented earlier in this chapter. An effective way to begin a reading and writing improvement class is with 15 to 20 minutes of uninterrupted sustained silent reading. This might be followed by another 15-minute segment during which learners read, either aloud or silently, their writings from a previous ses-

FIGURE 2.1 Form for Recording Attendance and Writings

Date Sessions   Stories
     Attended   Written

Name: _____

Starting Date : _____

Instructor: _____

Goal: _____

FIGURE 2.2 Form for Learners to Record Books Read

LIFELONG LEARNING CENTER

Books Read

Name _____

Instructor _____

Book Title   Date Completed

FIGURE 2.3 Form for Recording Spelling and Vocabulary Assessments

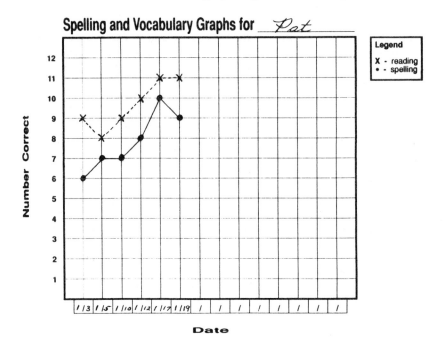

FIGURE 2.4 Form for Learners to Record Goals

LIFELONG LEARNING CENTER

Goals

Name _____

Date of entry into the Center _____

1. What are your goals for coming to the Center?

2. What are your goals now that you have been coming to the Center
   for _____ weeks?

---

sion. They might also participate in language activities related to these writings. Next, the class can work together on a reading or participate in a discussion guided by the teacher. Generally about 30 to 40 minutes is needed to read, examine, and discuss the day's topic. During the remaining 20 to 30 minutes, learners will write ideas and thoughts that have been stimulated by the reading and discussion. Attention to reading strategies, spelling, grammar, and other skills is interwoven throughout the class session. Specific suggestions and additional information about each of these four components of the lesson follow, with recommendations included for learners who are at beginning or low levels.

Uninterrupted Sustained Silent Reading

Learners select their reading material from the classroom library, with assistance from the teacher if necessary. The library contains a variety of reading materials with a wide range of difficulty. Occasionally the teacher may discuss the reading material informally with individuals. Most of the time, however, the teacher, too, is involved in silent reading, taking advantage of an opportunity to read and, more important, presenting a model and reinforcing the idea that reading practice is so valuable that class time is provided for it. A person who has minimal reading skills may read his or her stories or listen to a tape of those stories or other suitable material. Everyone must be viewed as a reader.

Practice Activities Based on Learners' Writings

Following the sustained silent reading, activities are planned around original materials written in previous lessons. When learners become comfortable, they can read aloud their materials. Such oral reading will be successful because the writings contain familiar ideas and language. Classmates will often raise questions, make comments, and compliment one another on their efforts. Everyone is encouraged to participate; however, if someone is embarrassed about reading aloud or if his or her writing is on a personal topic, a request not to participate should be respected.

Before the oral reading of these writings, the teacher may use vocabulary cards that have been developed from each learner's writing for a group activity, perhaps on root words, prefixes, synonyms, or categorization. Also, the teacher can develop individual exercises, based on each person's writings, to reinforce the learning of vocabulary; to work on spelling, contractions, and punctuation; or to focus on avoiding double negatives. The activities may be in the form of crossword puzzles (a computer software program makes this very easy), fill-in-the-blank passages, word associations, or matching exercises.

The vocabulary cards are made for words taken from the writing. No more than six misspelled words are selected from each writing. The words might be chosen either by the learner or by the teacher. Words that are important to the learner and that are used often in reading and writing are the best choices. The correctly spelled words are printed on index cards with a felt pen, one word per card. Lowercase letters should be used unless the word is a proper noun, in which case it should begin with a capital letter. A sentence, definition, picture, or other clue can be included. Learners file the cards alphabetically in their vocabulary boxes. At regular intervals, approximately every two weeks, each person is asked to write ten of these words. If the word can be spelled correctly, the assumption is that the word is known; if not, the word is repeated on the next list. These known words are re-tested occasionally, too, to ensure long-term learning. As a final step, the learner charts spelling progress by recording the number of words spelled correctly on the spelling graph in the manila record folder.

Guided Reading and Discussion

Following the sharing of stories and the related activities, a reading and discussion activity is held, which leads to the writing in the last phase of the lesson. Generally, a thought-provoking newspaper or magazine article, short story, editorial, public service brochure, or poem is used to trigger the discussion and to provide the content for the writing that will follow. Even though less able readers cannot read all of the text, they can certainly participate in the discussion and will be able to write about (or dictate to the teacher) their reactions to the topic and thus have material for subsequent reading activities. Alternatively, since this phase of the lesson serves as the stage of gathering and thinking about ideas for the writing phase, the trigger item might be a picture, cartoon, or short film rather than textual material. Issues or current events that the learners have heard about on radio or television can also serve as stimuli for discussion.

Whatever stimulus is used, plans must be made for the before, during, and after phases of this part of the lesson. Setting a purpose, predicting, asking questions, and summarizing are modeled and practiced with all trigger materials. In the paragraphs that follow, the assumption is that the learners are using printed materials, but the steps can be adapted to all other types of stimuli.

Before the actual reading, much attention should be given to getting the learners involved with the material and to establishing their purpose for reading it. Several minutes should be devoted to focusing on indicators of the content of the material, such as the title, words in boldface type, and visuals accompanying the text. Learners are encouraged to think about these and to relate them to information they have acquired previously from experience or from reading.

During the interaction with the text, learners read the material silently, one meaningful section at a time. A "meaningful section" implies a logical segment that is based on the structure of the material. For example, the identifiable parts of most stories are the setting, characters, problem or situation, episodes, and resolution of the problem. In expository materials, the headings and subheadings often indicate organization. Also it may be possible to distinguish patterns of organization within sections of text—enumerations or listings of information, compare–contrast, sequence, question–answer, and cause–effect—that will indicate meaningful points at which to stop and reflect.

As the learners read each section, they should be guided to become better readers by following certain steps: establishing a purpose for their reading, actively seeking information, thinking about whether the material is making sense, questioning frequently, making predictions, and visualizing. If unfamiliar words are encountered, help might be obtained from context clues, structural analysis, a dictionary, a thesaurus, or fellow learners. The emphasis is always on comprehension of the material rather than on the exact decoding of each word. Learners must experience the interactive nature of the reading process; they must become aware of strategies that are used to connect new information with the knowledge they already possess. Because many people may be unaware of the thought processes that occur during reading, the teacher might model and think aloud his or her interactions with the text.

Oral reading, discussion, questioning, and paraphrasing follow or are interspersed throughout the silent reading. The teacher might read aloud unless learners are anxious to do so. This might be done so less confident or less capable readers have an opportunity to follow the text while hearing the words. Listening to the passages read aloud may help everyone relate to and gain a better understanding of the material. Hearing the text also helps develop an appreciation for the flow and rhythm of the language. Even though the material will be read aloud, the silent reading should not be bypassed. With adequate preparation, learners will realize they can gain much from their silent reading. They will come to understand the importance of preparing for reading by getting an overview of the material and by setting a purpose for reading. As the learners become more proficient, oral reading will undoubtedly become more selective. Passages will be read by the teacher or the learners for specific purposes, such as to clarify points, pinpoint the author's techniques for indicating structure, share particularly humorous or thought-provoking parts, savor the language of well-turned phrases, or make some sense out of an unclear portion.

After the reading is completed, the teacher might ask for a summary of the article. Even more important than paraphrasing the author's writing, readers can be encouraged to share thoughts that have been triggered by the material, particularly thoughts about relationships of the information to their lives. These thoughts will become the basis for the writing that is to follow.

Because a number of strategies can be used to help the reader construct meaning by interacting with text, lessons could be confusing if every guided reading session were planned to incorporate several of them. Therefore, one strategy for improving reading or writing might be emphasized during each lesson, so the learners can become aware of how and why to use it. Although one strategy receives major attention during a given session, other appropriate strategies will be reinforced and practiced. For example, a short story might be used for the main purpose of helping learners establish the habit of predicting as they read; however, the strategies of visualizing and using context clues might also be appropriate during the same guided reading. Over a period of time, several techniques necessary for improved reading and writing will receive major attention in one lesson and then be incorporated in future sessions: previewing, skimming, scanning, using context clues, recognizing and interpreting descriptive or figurative language, recognizing the common ways of organizing informational articles, sequencing, summarizing, and comparing types of materials such as editorials and news articles.

For nonreaders, many of these strategies can be incorporated into listening and oral activities. For example, predicting and visualizing can be practiced even when the teacher reads the text aloud. The differences in style for front page news items and editorials can be discussed even by those who cannot yet read them independently. No matter what the trigger used—a film, picture, or speaker—the same techniques can be used by the teacher to get learners involved mentally so they enhance their background knowledge and retain substantive learning from the experience.

Of course, introducing a number of strategies as discrete techniques that must be learned along with their pedagogical terms (sequencing, skimming, scanning, using context clues) can be confusing. The reader needs an overall strategy for approaching texts, but does not necessarily need to know the pedagogical labels for the individual strategies. The 10 tips for improving comprehension in the following list, written in everyday language, might help teachers plan a logical sequence for introducing a general approach to texts. More important, the steps remind the reader of a sensible order of approaching text; the first six steps are natural ones to carry out before reading, and the last four will help during the reading. These tips might be displayed on a poster or printed on a bookmark for learners to use for reference as they move toward applying the strategies independently.

1. Read the title of the article. Think about its meaning or significance.
2. Look at pictures, maps, graphs, and charts related to the article. Read the captions. Try to think of situations similar to those illustrated.
3. Read paragraph headings and words in boldface type.
4. Think about the clues gained from steps 1–3; relate them to prior experience and knowledge.
5. Form questions about the article.
6. If there are questions at the end of the article or chapter, read them first.
7. Focus your mind on the material as you read. Actively seek information.
8. Vary your reading speed and strategies depending on your purpose for reading.
9. Be aware of what you're reading as you read.
10. Keep in mind the total picture.

Writing

In the final phase of the lesson, the learners write a story, essay, letter, or poem based on the thoughts stimulated by the guided reading and discussion. Now the content of the lesson becomes even more personalized and meaningful for the learners. Adults have large oral vocabularies; moreover, they have had innumerable experiences that give them ideas about which to write. The guided reading and discussion phase of the lesson has spurred their thinking about some of those experiences. Many learners find it challenging to record their thoughts. In fact, some may feel they are unable to do so at first, and the teacher will need to provide support on an individual basis. If the person begins to show frustration, the teacher might provide a gentle reminder of particular points that struck a spark of interest during the discussion and prompt him or her to elaborate on one of them. Most adults have not encountered this method of teaching previously and may need such prompts at the early stages, but after an introduction to it they respond favorably. The majority soon overcome their reluctance and inhibitions and begin to write. They find it exciting and rewarding to record their thoughts and feelings and to share what they have written with others.

To assist with getting started and with organizing ideas, the clustering technique may be used (Rico, 1983). Clustering is an excellent pre-writing activity that involves brainstorming and associating ideas around a central concept and portraying those ideas in graphic form. The technique will be beneficial for all learners. It is a powerful tool for getting reluctant writers to feel they are capable of writing. It works equally well with learners who are more confident; for them it serves as a way of organizing their thoughts prior to writing. Clustering can be used to generate ideas for any kind of narrative or expository writing—letters, reports, short stories, poems, or articles. It leads to natural, expressive writing. For most people, putting ideas on paper in this random, clustering fashion is less inhibiting than staring at a blank page with the implausible expectation that the most effective way to begin is simply to start writing sentences. Clustering truly helps many adults overcome the negative attitudes they have about writing.

Not only is clustering helpful, it is easy to teach and learn. When a person has decided on a topic, the central idea is jotted down in the center of a sheet of paper. The idea may be expressed in a single word or a short phrase. It is circled and becomes the nucleus for the cluster. Then the writer brainstorms on that word or idea, as shown in the example about money in Figure 2.5. The learner should be encouraged to think of relationships, to make connections, and to let his or her ideas flow, making sure to write each idea on the paper. The words can be arranged randomly or

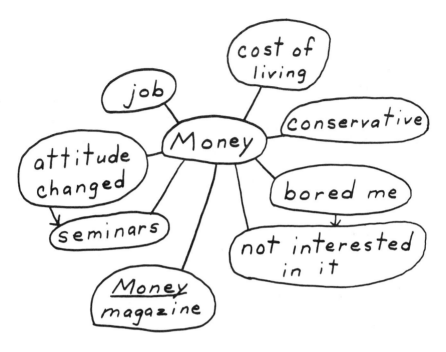

FIGURE 2.5   An Example of Clustering Around Topic of Money

they can radiate outward from the nucleus. Each new idea is circled and a line is drawn connecting it to the central topic. Some words or ideas may be connected to a secondary word rather than to the nucleus. Arrows may be used to indicate the association or relationship of ideas. Bright colored pencils or felt pens may be used to indicate secondary topics or categories. After a few minutes the person will have developed a pattern or network of thoughts related to the main topic.

The learner now has vocabulary, ideas, and even a sense of organization to help with the writing process. At this point, he or she may find it helpful to write a focusing statement to provide a sense of direction for the writing. Most people can now write with much more confidence because the anxiety about what to say and how to start has been relieved. Another possible source of anxiety must be alleviated, however; the writer must be helped to realize that it is not necessary to use every word or idea generated through the clustering. Only the information that relates to and makes sense in the planned piece need be used. In the brainstorming process, some irrelevant words or phrases may have been included. Some of the thoughts must be ignored in order to have well-focused writing. When clustering is introduced, teacher modeling of the technique and the thinking involved in selecting and using the clustered ideas might be very helpful.

Learners are encouraged to write freely, to let their thoughts flow on the paper. During this writing, the emphasis is on content, not mechanics. Use of the dictionary to obtain correct spellings is discouraged as this impedes the writing process. Instead, writers are encouraged to "spell as best you can, so you don't lose your idea." Writing on every other line will allow space for the next steps of revising and editing.

When the draft is finished, the revision process is carried out jointly by the teacher and the learner. The focus during revision is still on the content of the material. Does it say what the writer intended? Does it make sense? Are events in a logical sequence? If the class has 10 learners, obviously the teacher must be aware of each writer's progress in order to be available to assist when the revision stage is reached; fortunately not everyone will reach it at the same time. The early writing efforts of less able readers and writers will often be rather short, so the needed individual conference can take place fairly quickly. If some of the learners write longer pieces, this may be an indication of more confidence and thus probably more ability to go ahead with their own revising. Once the camaraderie of the class has been established, writers may turn to fellow learners as sounding boards regarding content.

Editing, or proofreading, is next. The learner and teacher together improve sentence construction, identify misspelled words, and correct punctuation. The changes are noted on the draft; the material is not always rewritten by the learner. Figure 2.6 is an edited draft developed around the clustering example on money.

Before the next class session, the teacher can prepare duplicate, quadruple-spaced typewritten copies of the revised and edited version. One copy is placed in the learner's colored folder for use in subsequent lessons. On the second copy, the learner can rewrite the material beneath the typed lines, paying attention to the punctuation, capitalization, and spelling as a means of internalizing the conventions of writing. During the initial writing, the emphasis is on content; during the rewriting, the emphasis is on mechanics—but mechanics as a means of clarifying the meaning. After a story has been rewritten, the teacher looks it over. The learner keeps this copy in a personalized folder for future reread-

FIGURE 2.6   An Edited Draft Based on Money Cluster

Money: $\overset{N}{\text{No}}$ $\overset{L}{\text{longer}}$ $\overset{B}{\text{boring}}$

I used to say money
bored me. It wasn't
because it's so $\overset{\text{I had}}{}$ much of
it; its just that I
$\overset{\text{really}}{\cancel{\text{realy}}}$ didn't care $\overset{\text{to}}{}$ think
about it. ~~I started~~

~~reading Money magazine~~
~~recently.~~ I wasn't
interested in budgeting
it, in reading $\overset{\text{about}}{}$ it or in
making it "grow" by
investing it. $\overset{A}{\text{Recently}}$, my
$\overset{\text{attitude}}{\cancel{\text{atitude}}}$ about money
has changed. Now I'm
interested in $\overset{\text{learning}}{\cancel{\text{terning}}}$
about it; so I've
attended a couple of one-
day seminars on $\overset{\text{personal}}{\cancel{\text{personal}}}$

(Continued)

FIGURE 2.6 *Continued*

finance. In the future, I plan to take an adult education class dealing with money management. Since my daughter was aware of my new interest in this area, she gave me an appropriate gift at Christmastime. Under the tree was a Christmas card, indicating I would begin receiving *Money* magazine in January. I've discovered that learning about money is far from boring. Instead, I've found money to be a fascinating, complex subject.

ing or rewriting away from the class setting. The typed and rewritten version of the article about money is shown in Figure 2.7.

VARIATIONS WITHIN THE LESSON FORMAT

The four-part instructional format provides the context for helping learners interact with information and recognize its relevance to their lives. While the phases of the lesson remain fairly constant, the content and activities within those phases provide variety. Because information and lives are continually changing, the teacher needs to be alert to selecting current materials. The use of appropriate materials is crucial to the success of the program. A wide range of materials representing different types of reading must be used, not only for variety but to help learners adapt strategies to the type of text. In addition to varied materials, adults enjoy being challenged in new ways and they respond enthusiastically to variations on the learning activities.

Some ideas for materials for the guided reading and discussion phase of the lesson follow. Many of these suggest variations for the writing for the day as well. Some of the suggestions are appropriate for group activities, while others can be used for individual practice. Some are suitable for guided reading and discussion, while others offer alternatives for the writing phase. Whatever the variation, it should be related to the topic for the day.

- Read articles on the same topic but with increasing levels of difficulty from publications such as *News for You* (New Readers Press), the daily newspaper, and *Time* magazine; the fact that the more difficult articles will seem easier after reading other related information will help readers get a sense of the importance of prior knowledge.
- Interpret newspaper political cartoons; determine the opinion of the cartoonist; discuss and write about feelings on the topic.
- Compare an editorial or a letter to the editor with a political cartoon, possibly ones with contrasting opinions; the learners might try their hand at writing a letter to the editor on the topic.
- Compare and analyze an editorial and a news article on the same topic, for example, the 65-mile-per-hour speed limit or the use of radar detectors.
- Read narrative and expository texts on the same topic; for ex-

FIGURE 2.7   Final Version of Writing on Money

Money: No Longer Boring

Money: No Longer Boring

I used to say money bored me.   It wasn't

I used to say money bored me. It wasn't

because I had so much of it;   it's just that I

because I had so much of it; it's just that I

really didn't care to think about it.   I wasn't

really didn't care to think about it. I wasn't

interested in budgeting it, in reading about it or

interested in budgeting it, in reading about it or

in making it "grow" by investing it.

in making it "grow" by investing it.

Recently, my attitude about money has changed.

Recently, my attitude about money has changed.

Now I'm interested in learning about it, so I've

Now I'm interested in learning about it, so I've

attended a couple of one-day seminars on personal

attended a couple of one-day seminars on personal

finance.   In the future, I plan to take an adult

finance. In the future, I plan to take an adult

education class dealing with money management.

education class dealing with money management.

Since my daughter was aware of my new interest

Since my daughter was aware of my new interest

in this area, she gave me an appropriate gift at

in this area, she gave me an appropriate gift at

Christmastime. Under the tree was a Christmas card

Christmastime. Under the tree was a Christmas card

indicating I would begin receiving <u>Money</u> magazine

indicating I would begin receiving <u>Money</u> magazine

in January.

in January.

I've discovered that learning about money is

I've discovered that learning about money is

far from boring. Instead, I've found money to be a

far from boring. Instead, I've found money to be a

fascinating, complex subject.

fascinating, complex subject.

---

ample, an article about the effects of cocaine and a narrative, perhaps a first-person account of addiction.

• Compare two versions of a short story, emphasizing visualization and having learners discuss the effects on imagery when descriptive phrases are omitted or altered in the rewritten form. Use rewritten classics or prepare materials such as those described in the Literature and the Arts lesson in Chapter 3.

• Use quotations, famous or not-so-famous, on specific topics—money, marriage, children—as a springboard for the discussion and writing for the day; quotations might also be used when introducing a story or an article.

• Use a poem or short story that contains descriptive, figurative language to encourage visualizing, for example, "Polar Night" (Burke, 1970), "A Christmas Memory" (Capote, 1980), and "Southbound on the Freeway" (Swenson, 1986).

• Use a poem or short story to show the effectiveness of appropriate speech patterns or dialect, such as in "Mother to Son" (Hughes, 1967) or "A Good Little Feature" (Blackman, 1970).

Strategies that can be used to enhance the reader's interaction with printed materials before, during, or after reading include:

- Preview as a means of getting an overview of an article in a short time.
- Skim or scan quickly to gain vocabulary and ideas from a short article.
- Apply the sqrrr (survey, question, read, recite, review) strategy—survey pictures, headings, introductions, and summaries; raise questions based on the subheadings; read a section at a time to answer the questions; recite the answers to the questions at the end of each section; and, at the end, recall and review the overall organization and important points. A "P" or "predict" phase might be included between "question" and "read" to involve readers in activating background knowledge and anticipating possible answers to the questions.
- Use a mapping technique to recall information from an article read previously, then read a more difficult article on the same topic and add to the map. (Mapping is described and illustrated in Chapter 3.)
- Map an article read during the first week in class; refer to it again after several weeks to see how the map helps in recalling information.
- Map a short story with a focus on character descriptions or the sequence of events.
- Type an article with some of the key words deleted, to help learners use context clues.

Writing practice is as important as reading practice. Opportunities can be provided in the lesson for independent self-directed writing, similar to uninterrupted sustained silent reading. Learners might keep journals in which they write each time they come to class. They can spend a few minutes recording any ideas about which they have been thinking, perhaps related to work, the weather, or their family activities. These journals should remain confidential unless the learner wants to share or seeks help with what has been written. Learners must be helped to understand that even though these journals are not corrected, the writing done in them will be beneficial and will help them grow in their ability to write more easily and fluently. Writing in these journals will help to improve the thinking processes that precede writing, aid in the ability to organize materials, and continue the development of skills involved in conveying thoughts and ideas more coherently in writing.

If a learner has difficulty getting started with the journal writing, suggest that he or she record just that dilemma. For example, the entry might be, "I can't think of anything to write about today. My mind is a blank. Maybe I am too tired to write. I hope next time I'm in class I can think of something to write about." In this case, the learner is still practicing writing, even though the content is lacking in substance.

Journals can be prepared easily by putting lined looseleaf notebook paper in colored folders. Affix a label with the words, "My Free Writing Journal," and the writer's name to the front of each folder and keep the journal in the manila folder described previously.

In addition to this free writing, specific writing activities can be planned to provide practice on a particular type of text structure and help learners elaborate on their ideas:

• Write descriptive or compare–contrast articles based on two similar items (coffee mugs, model cars).
• Use "Wordless Workshop" pages from *Popular Science* magazine as exercises on the importance of logical sequencing.
• Write a description of an object that has been felt but not seen (such as a tool or a decorative object), then write another description of the same object when it can be seen; this helps learners realize the importance of knowledge gained through experience, observation, or reading before writing on a topic.
• Cluster before writing, or write first and then cluster in order to expand the article.
• Use cartoons, preferably those with no words, from the Sunday newspaper, over a three-period lesson. On the first day, write one descriptive sentence for each frame. On the second day, imagine and write the conversation in each frame. On the third day, use the corrected descriptive sentences and dialogue to write a story of the cartoon strip, incorporating as much or as little of the first two assignments as desired.

Activities for practicing specific skills can be varied and interesting as well. For example,

• Choose or write a short humorous story containing dialogue. Type it with no punctuation or paragraphing and have the learners discuss the readability of it. Compare it with the same story typed with no punctuation but paragraphed correctly. Have the learners decide what punctuation and paragraphing are needed and then compare the original version with their corrected version.

- To help with paragraph organization, choose or prepare a paragraph. Write each sentence from it on a separate index card. Have learners arrange the sentences in the correct sequence. If the sentences could be arranged in more than one way, discuss the possibilities and determine which would be best.
- Do a similar exercise using a short article. Write each paragraph on a separate card and have learners arrange them in the best order.
- Use cartoons for sequencing and predicting. Laminate and cut apart each frame of the cartoons. Give each person one of the cartoons minus the last frame. Ask the learners to arrange their cartoon strip in a logical sequence and predict what happened in the last frame.
- Have learners visualize the correct spelling of a word they misspelled—see it as a neon light.
- Have learners print an especially troublesome word on an index card using a bright colored marker. Suggest they tape it to the refrigerator door, bathroom mirror, or some other place where they will see it frequently.
- Have learners write difficult vocabulary or spelling words in a shoebox lid containing a layer of salt or sand.

Many of the materials that people write merit a wider audience than their peers in the class. Publication of materials is a fine way to help learners feel good about their efforts. In addition to the possibility of submitting letters to the editor, some local newspapers have a weekly column in which they publish articles from their readers. Another way to "get into print" is to publish a newspaper or magazine that contains a collection of learners' writings on a particular topic, such as "An Automobile Anthology."

ILLUSTRATIVE LESSON PLAN

The first 15 to 20 minutes of any lesson will be devoted to uninterrupted sustained silent reading. Oral reading and other activities related to writings from previous sessions will follow. In the lesson that follows, Stephen Crane's (1968) short story, "A Dark Brown Dog," is used to show one way of developing the third phase of the lesson, guided reading and discussion, and of relating it to the fourth phase, writing.

Lesson Objectives.   In this lesson, learners will

- gain appreciation for the short story form
- use prediction as a means of getting involved with a good short story
- use imaging (getting a picture in one's mind of the sights, sounds, and feelings) to help make a story come alive and to aid retention
- relate the situation in the story to situations in today's society

Materials.   The short story, "A Dark Brown Dog," by Stephen Crane (1968). Stopping points for discussion should be indicated by dots in the text (see Figure 2.8).

Procedure.   Introduce the story by giving brief biographical information about Stephen Crane. Information (which can be readily obtained from an encyclopedia) might include such facts as: He was an American novelist, journalist, war correspondent, and poet who was born in 1871; he was probably most famous for his Civil War novel, *The Red Badge of Courage,* written in 1895; he died in Germany of tuberculosis in 1900. Given that background information, readers might be surprised to find a short story by Crane, and learners can be asked to ponder what he might write about in a short story entitled "A Dark Brown Dog." After the learners discuss the title and the possibilities, explain that the story is based on the relationships between the dog, a boy, and his family, especially his father. Ask students to predict the feelings that might be expressed in the story.

Have learners read silently to the first dot, which marks the spot the teacher has selected for the first stopping point. Suggest that as they read they try to visualize the setting and the child (age, appearance, feelings) and try to imagine the sounds in the neighborhood.

Read to the second dot, visualizing the dog and the boy's reactions to it. After reading the section, ask questions related to these imagings: Is the dog a puppy? Is he a stray? How does the dog feel about the boy? How does the boy feel about the dog? Why did the boy strike the dog on the head?

Continue reading to the third dot. Can you see the dog "praying" to the child? Why did the author choose the word "praying"?

Read to the next dot. How does the boy treat the dog? Why

(text continues on p. 45)

FIGURE 2.8 Text for Guided Reading and Discussion ("A Dark Brown Dog")

a dark brown dog

By Stephen Crane

A child stood on a street corner. He leaned against a fence and kicked at the ground.

Sunshine beat down on the pavement, and trucks clattered down the avenue. The child stood and dreamed.●

After a time a little dark brown dog came trotting down the sidewalk. A short rope was dragging from his neck. Sometimes he walked on the end of it and stumbled.

He stopped opposite the child, and they looked at each other. The dog wagged his tail. The child put out his hand and called to him. In a shy way the dog came near the boy, and the two greeted each other with pats and wags. The dog got more excited with each minute, until he almost knocked the boy over with his friendliness. Then the child lifted his hand and struck the dog on the head.●

This seemed to amaze the little dark brown dog, and hurt him to the heart. He fell down helplessly at the child's feet. When the child hit him again, and screamed at him, he turned over on his back and held his paws up. He seemed to be praying to the child.

The child thought he looked funny lying on his back and holding his paws that way. The boy laughed, and kept hitting the dog so he would stay in that position. But the dog took it all very seriously, and kept pleading with the boy to forgive him.●

Finally the child got bored with this game and started for home. The dog was still praying. He lay on his back and watched the boy as he walked away.

Soon he got to his feet and started after the child as he wandered slowly home. The child stopped for a moment, and saw that the little dark brown dog was following him like a shadow.

The child found a small stick and beat the dog. The dog lay down and prayed until the child finished beating him and started for home again. The dog got up and followed him.

On the way home, the child turned many times and beat the dog, telling him that he thought he was worthless and no good to anyone. The dog seemed anxious to make up for being so useless, and continued to follow the boy.●

When the child reached his door, the dog was still right behind him. The child sat down on his stoop and the two of them began to play. The dog did everything he could to please the child. In fact, he was so funny that the boy suddenly realized the dog would be a wonderful toy after all. He grabbed for the dog's rope.

He dragged the animal into the hall and up the long dark stairways. The dog tried to follow, but he could not run very easily up the stairs; the boy moved so quickly that the dog became frightened. In his mind he was being dragged to a terrible but unknown fate. His eyes grew wild with terror. He tried to run away.

The child dragged even harder and they had a

battle on the stairs. The child won because he put in so much effort, and because the dog was very small. The boy dragged his new toy to the door of his home. The two went inside.

No one was there. The child sat down on the floor and began to play with the dog, who cheered up at once. He licked his new companion, and soon they were the best of friends. ●

When the child's family arrived, they started fighting immediately. They looked at the dog and cursed him. Everyone hated him. The dog felt their anger and began to droop like a plant without water. The boy walked over to the dog and screamed at the top of his voice that the dog was his and that everyone should leave them alone.

In the middle of all the screaming, the father arrived home. He wanted to know what the hell they were making the kid scream for. They told him that the damn kid wanted this horrible dog to live with them.

They all began shouting at once, but the fight was over quickly. The father was in a rage that night, and when he saw that everybody else would be angry and miserable if the dog was allowed to stay, he decided that the dog should definitely stay. The child, crying softly, took his friend into another room, while the father screamed at his wife. And that was how the dog entered the family. ●

The boy and the dog were together every minute of the day and night. The child became his protector and friend. If the grownups kicked the dog, or threw things at him, the child screamed at them to stop. Once, in the middle of a fight, the child had run to the dog, yelling, with tears pouring down his face, and his arms stretched out to protect his friend. He was struck in the head with a huge pot which his father had thrown at the dog because the dog annoyed him. After that, the others were a little more careful when they threw things at the dog. The dog also became very clever at dodging things the family threw at him, so that even when things did hit him, they didn't hurt him too badly.

The family didn't dare to try anything too cruel in front of the child because he would make such a loud and angry fuss that he was unbearable. In this way he protected the dog.

But the child could not always be there. At night, when he was asleep, his dark brown friend would get up and cry with loneliness. At these times the family would chase him all over the kitchen and hit him with anything they could get their hands on.

When the child was very sad, he would crawl under the table and lay his head on the dog's back. The dog would always make him feel better.

In time, the dog grew. He developed a loud bark, which seemed almost magic coming from such a small dog. He stopped crying at night.

He loved the boy more and more as time went on. He would wag his tail when the boy entered the house, and cry when the boy left. He could tell the sound of the boy's steps from all the other noises of the neighborhood, and it was like a voice calling to him. He loved the boy with perfect love.

The child used to go on little trips to explore the neighborhood and usually his friend jogged along behind him. The dog felt that these were very impor-

(Continued)

FIGURE 2.8 *Continued*

tant trips, and he would carry himself with the air of a proud servant serving a great king. ●

One day the father went out and got drunk. He came home and began throwing pots and pans and furniture at his wife. He was in the middle of this "game" when the child came in, followed by his dog. They were returning from one of their trips.

The child, from long experience, could tell at once that his father was in one of his moods. The boy ran under the table, which he knew was usually a safe place. The dog had less experience with the father. He thought that running under the table meant "here's a new game," and started to patter across the floor to join the boy. He was the picture of a little dark brown dog on the way to see a friend.

At this moment the father saw him. He gave a huge howl of joy and knocked the dog down with a heavy coffee-pot. The dog yelled in surprise and pain and ran to hide. The man kicked out with his heavy foot, making the dog stagger. A second blow with the coffee-pot knocked him to the floor.

The child began screaming, and ran out from under the table to protect his dog. The father paid no attention to the crying child, and continued to beat the dog. After he was knocked down two more times, the dog simply gave up. He rolled over on his back and held his paws up in his praying way. ●

But the father was in a mood for fun, and it seemed to him that it would be the most fun of all to throw the dog out the window. So he reached down and grabbed the dog by the leg and lifted him up. He swung him two or three times around his head, laughing all the while, and threw him out the window.

This event caused great surprise on the street. A man looked up to watch the flying dog. Children ran shouting. A woman watering plants across the alley dropped a flower-pot.

The dark brown body crashed in a heap on the roof of a shed five stories below. From there it rolled to the pavement of an alley.

The child upstairs howled with pain, and ran from the room. It took him a long time to reach the alley because he was too small to run down the stairs.

When they came for him later, they found him seated by the body of his dark brown friend. ●

Source: Crane, S. (1968). A dark brown dog. In *Uptight, the name of the game.* Jericho, NY: New Dimensions in Education. Originally published by Random House, from the public domain.

does he beat him with a stick? How does the dog react? In what way are the words "he thought he was worthless and no good to anyone" significant? Why did the dog continue to follow the boy?

Continue reading to the next dot. Can you think of an appropriate way to change the sentence, "The dog did everything he could to please the child"? Can you see the dog being dragged up the stairs? What kind of building are you visualizing? Why did the boy take the dog home? Will the boy be allowed to keep the dog?

Read silently to the next dot. Describe the family members and their reaction to the dog. Could you see the dog "droop like a plant without water"? Who gave permission for the dog to stay? Why? Why did the father act the way he did? Will the dog become the family pet?

Read to the next dot. What kind of feelings developed between the boy and the dog? What did each do for the other? What kind of influence did the child and dog exert on the family? If you were asked to write an ending for this story, what would it be?

Again, read to the next dot. As you read, try to visualize the father, the boy, and the dog. Try to hear the sounds in the apartment that day. What will happen to the boy? To the dog? What might the father do next? If you lived in a neighboring apartment and heard the commotion, what would you do?

Read to the end of the story. Could you see the neighborhood reacting to the event? Were you with the boy as he went down the stairs? How will this event affect the relationship between the boy and his father? Were the feelings between the boy and his dog natural or exaggerated?

Did you think the story would end in this way? Could this story have happened? Have you ever witnessed anything similar to this? If so, can you see it in your mind now? Can you feel your reactions?

After the learners have read the story silently, section by section, followed by questioning and discussion, the teacher can read the selection aloud from beginning to end, if desired, encouraging the listeners to visualize the characters and the events once more. To help the learners realize the importance of predicting and evaluating, a moment or two might be spent on having them comment about the values of anticipating what will happen and of imaging during the story.

Then the learners will be asked to write thoughts that have been triggered by "A Dark Brown Dog." Since imaging was the main activity emphasized during the reading, that might be carried over to the writing. Before writing, each person might be encouraged to recall his or her visualizations and feelings about similar episodes. Many might be inspired to write about the impact of parents' behavior on their children. Whatever direction they take, they might be encouraged to use those imagings as they write. As can be seen, both the content and the strategies used during the guided reading can be influential in the writing phase.

SUMMARY: READING, WRITING, AND SELF–ESTEEM

Whole language provides a framework for instruction that is characterized by the use of complete texts and group interaction and that builds on the relationships between reading and writing. In this chapter, a format showing how a whole language framework is implemented in reading and writing classes has been described. First the learners read texts of their selection during sustained silent reading. Next they share materials that they have written in a previous session and practice skills appropriate to their needs. Then they are guided to discuss a relevant topic or interact with interesting whole texts selected by the teacher as vehicles for helping them learn and apply reading strategies. They discuss and listen to one another respond to the topic or the text, bringing their own experiences to bear as they construct new meanings about the subject. Finally they write their thoughts and feelings about the subject for the day.

The techniques explained in this chapter are effective ones that can be incorporated into any reading and writing improvement program for adults, whether they are learning in groups or through individual tutoring and whether they enter the program as nonreaders or with some skills. This positive approach is based on a natural progression of successful reading and writing experiences. The methods work because they build on what the learner already knows, thus increasing self-confidence and self-esteem. The respect demonstrated by the teacher and the learners toward one another enhances the feeling of self-respect, which is so essential to learning.

≪ 3 ≫

The GED Connection

Teachers involved in a GED program proceed on the conviction that people who enroll in classes are capable of learning and successfully completing work toward receiving a high school equivalency certificate. Adults come with a rich store of life experiences and the desire to learn. For years they may have wanted to get their diplomas, but the demands of work and home or the reluctance about returning to a formal educational setting after a long period of time outweighed that desire. With the emergence of technological changes and the emphasis on education in the workplace, many decide to channel the time, energy, and determination needed to work toward their GED certificates. Some may have doubts about being able to succeed in school; nonetheless, they have taken that important first step of enrolling, thus exhibiting a willingness to try. Those who enter the program must often balance heavy responsibilities with the difficult task of studying the five areas of GED: Literature and the Arts, Social Studies, Science, Mathematics, and Writing.

Because of the many pressures on learners, a successful GED program must be designed to maintain and extend their motivation. The teacher must encourage learners to attend classes regularly and praise them when they do so. The classroom should be a disciplined but comfortable environment, in which there is a partnership between the teacher and learners to maximize learning. Learners feel free to ask questions and express their ideas in this cooperative atmosphere. The teacher strives for clarity and brevity in presenting, expanding, and reinforcing lessons from the GED textbooks, with most of the time spent on teacher–learner interaction rather than teacher lecturing.

Learners are kept as actively involved with the material as possible. The teacher assumes that adults already know some of the information in the readings or graphics and can certainly apply experiences they have had to the concepts. The first task is to bring that knowledge to the surface by having the learners question, talk about what they already know, and predict the information they may find. When they read, they should be alert to confirm their predictions and pick up new information. After reading, they will want to share what they have learned and think about it together, applying it to their experiences.

Writing is done across all phases of the curriculum. Most people come with minimal writing experience. Since a writing sample is required to receive a GED certificate, it is essential for learners to begin writing as soon as possible in a GED program. Beyond this obvious practical reason to include writing as an ongoing part of the program, writing, like discussion and reading, enables learners to reach a higher level of thinking (Jensen, 1984; Pearson & Tierney, 1984; Rubin & Hansen, 1986). Writing enables people to process and understand content material better. Also, as Van Nostrand (1979) has said, writing means discovery. Each time we write, we are gaining new information, creating new thoughts, and becoming more aware of ourselves.

Class time is set aside for independent reading and writing. Few adults are able to do much of this at home because of time constraints, although they are encouraged to do so.

The learners also take an active role in evaluating their progress. First they set goals and work toward them. Every eight to ten weeks they review their goals as they consider what they have learned, how they feel about learning, and how that has made a difference in their lives. In any educational program a growing confidence is the most powerful factor in stimulating an individual toward progress. The teacher must foster this feeling by praising individual learners for working hard and moving ahead, as well as asking them to evaluate themselves with a positive eye.

A major objective of those enrolled in a GED program is, of course, to pass the GED tests. Besides learning reading and writing strategies and the required curriculum for the five areas, the learners must prepare for test-taking. Accordingly, learners should have experiences in class visualizing their success in the test situation, relaxing before and during the tests, and practicing tests from textbooks and the GED Test Center. The practice tests are viewed as opportunities for learning, and after each test the learner and teacher together assess the responses and review the information in the items. As soon as both feel the learner is ready to go to the GED Test Center to take the actual test, the teacher assists him or her in making the appointment.

While passing the tests is a powerful incentive, it is an extrinsic reward. Learners in a GED program need to feel capable and challenged; teachers must ensure that the program meets this intrinsic need. The way in which class sessions are organized is an important factor in fulfilling this need and is described in the section that follows. Using a whole language framework to promote learning in the five areas works well, and overall guidelines for applying the principles to GED sessions are presented next. These principles are then applied to five specific illustrative lessons, one for each of the GED areas: Literature and the Arts, Social Studies, Science, Mathematics, and Writing.

ORGANIZATION OF GED CLASS SESSIONS

When adults enter the program, they need an overview of what is entailed and they should be involved in deciding where to begin. They are shown the textbooks and receive a brief explanation of the main areas of study and the class procedure. Most people should start with one of the two basic areas—Literature and the Arts (reading) or Mathematics—but the decision should be theirs. The teacher may strongly recommend that they begin with reading, because a solid foundation in that component is most helpful for all subjects. However, if a person expresses a firm desire to study math first, the teacher abides by this decision. The teacher also recommends that learners work on the writing textbook last, after they have engaged in writing as an integral part of lessons in the other subjects.

Once the beginning area for study has been determined, the teacher and the learner collaborate on an initial informal assessment. For reading, the individual is asked for his or her perceptions about being able to handle the material in the literature book. If the material is felt to be far too difficult, a reading and writing improvement course, described in Chapter 2, will be recommended before beginning the GED material. For math, representative problems on the pre-test are shown and the learner is asked about the level of confidence in the four basic operations of addition, subtraction, multiplication, and division. If the feeling is that a review of them would be advisable, the pre-test is omitted at this time and instruction begins. If, on the other hand, the learner seems ready to take the pre-test, assurance is given that the reason for the test is to determine what material to review or introduce.

Most adults perceive tests as indications of their inadequacies and are thus very anxious about tests; they rarely see tests as means for determining needs and avoiding repetition of lessons on material that is already known.

Although adults come with a wide range of experience, they benefit from the support of and involvement with other learners in group settings, as explained in Chapter 1. Once they take the step to seek assistance, instruction should begin as soon as possible to take advantage of this commitment. This means, of course, that in GED programs where the number of adults is too small to have on-going separate classes for each subject, the areas of study and the pace of learning for members in the group will vary widely. Although instruction and study within the group are often on a one-to-one basis, those who are studying the same subject will have guided group discussions on teacher-selected topics so they can benefit from the flow of ideas generated by the group.

If it can be arranged, learners should come twice a week for one-and-one-half-hour classes. Meeting regularly takes advantage of the benefits of spaced learning without too much time intervening between sessions. Although learners are progressing individually, so that it might seem that a missed class would make no difference, the teacher should try to schedule makeup sessions for classes missed. This reinforces the seriousness of the endeavor. If someone doesn't come to class and hasn't given a reason, the teacher should mail a reminder, make a phone call, or see the person on the job if the classes are conducted at the workplace. This persuasive communication and the availability of the teacher for makeup sessions help the learner realize the importance of attendance and the caring of the teacher.

Adults can continue taking classes as long as it takes them to complete their GEDs. If they set realistic target dates for each test and work consistently toward their goals, their continued attainment of successful steps will encourage them to fulfill their requirements as soon as possible.

APPLYING WHOLE LANGUAGE PRINCIPLES TO GED

Although the ultimate outcome of GED classes is that adults pass the tests, the focus must be on learning to learn; the real goal is that people become independent, confident learners. To determine whether this goal actually underlies a GED program, one needs only

to observe the extent to which attention is given to guiding learners to acquire strategies for constructing meaning and applying
knowledge—as contrasted with providing them with "interesting"
lessons so that the content will be remembered. In other words, is
the focus on the learner or on the content? Is it on the process or on
the material? When GED lessons are centered on the learner and the
process of learning, not only will the necessary information be acquired, but the individual will be launched on a lifelong learning
journey. Thus, GED preparation should be provided within a whole
language framework in which reading and writing strategies are
used as tools for learning in all areas of study.

Reading Strategies

As in all effective reading instruction, the focus in GED reading is on
constructing meaning and applying that meaning to one's life.
Learners must think about the material in any subject before, during, and after reading in order to get meaning from the text, construct new thoughts, and apply the insights to their experience.
These strategies are the same as those described for reading and
writing improvement classes in Chapter 2; GED learners apply
them at higher levels.
     Before reading, learners should think about what they already
know about the topic. They should read the title, scan the reading
selection, and look at headings and graphic aids to gain an awareness of the main ideas and the overall organization of the material.
They can predict some of the information that might be presented
and, as they predict, they will undoubtedly realize that they bring
a lot of information to the page. Teachers can use a variety of pre-
reading activities to spark interest. For example, learners might be
asked to anticipate some of the vocabulary that might occur in a
passage on a given topic. The teacher, or better yet the learners,
might raise questions about the topic. All readers should have a
purpose for approaching a text, and that purpose should be determined by the learner rather than by the teacher if the person is to
become an independent interactive reader.
     As people read, they should think about the content. They
should ask themselves questions about the material. They can visualize the characters, scene, action, or information. They might
relate the ideas to their experiences. With expository text, learners
might want to jot down key concepts as they read. If they come to
an unfamiliar word, they can use context, word structure, or phon-

ics clues to figure it out; however, if these strategies do not work and the word is not absolutely essential to the meaning, they can go on reading and return to it later. Many adults do not automatically use these strategies during reading, so it may be necessary for the teacher to model and provide guided practice with them.

After reading, learners should be asked to look back to their predictions and see whether ideas should be added or revised based on information from the text. To help them remember and apply the information, other post-reading activities can be used. Some techniques are particularly appropriate for the content areas, such as Social Studies and Science. One useful post-reading technique for organizing and retaining content material is mapping, which is a graphic representation of main ideas, details, and connections among the concepts (Heimlich & Pittelman, 1986). Many readers find that a visual portrayal of the material clarifies its overall organization. Although there is no right or wrong way to create a map, the major headings should be clearly distinguishable. Lines are drawn to connect supporting details to major concepts so that the focus is on relationships and associations rather than isolated bits of information. Since mapping will be unfamiliar to many adults, the teacher will need to model and provide guided practice with it. Figure 3.1 shows a map developed to help readers get a sense of the relationships of the many facts presented in the section of the GED science text shown in Figure 3.2.

Discussions of related materials are also important post-reading activities. The use of text, diagrams, and pictures in supplementary materials will add depth to the topic and provide opportunities for learners to compare and evaluate sources of information. The teacher should keep a file of articles, pictures, graphs, and political cartoons from newspapers and magazines, and the file should be updated continually so the materials are always current. (The lessons on science and social studies in this chapter were appropriate at the time the book was written, but the materials are illustrative only; the techniques must be adapted to up-to-date materials each time the class is taught.)

For another post-reading technique, the teacher can prepare open-ended questions or objective-type items (such as multiple-choice questions), which the learners will read before approaching the printed material and discuss afterwards. These questions are best if they alert readers to focus on main ideas, inferences, or a logical line of thought rather than random facts. The following dis-

FIGURE 3.1 Mapping for a Portion of a Science Text

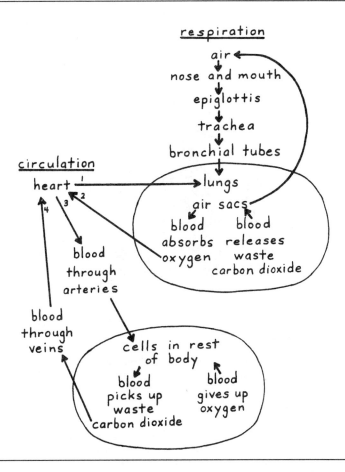

cussion questions for articles on scientific study are based on the
logic of the scientific method:

- Describe the problem addressed in the article. What was the
  main goal of the scientists?
- Can you state the hypothesis the study was based on? What facts
  did the researchers have before the study? What did they think
  the results of their study would be?
- What are the methods the scientists used to explore the prob-

FIGURE 3.2 Science Text for the Mapping Example

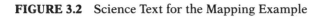

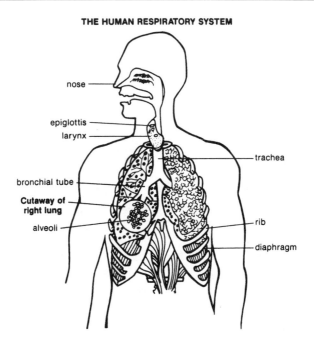

THE HUMAN RESPIRATORY SYSTEM

   In order to get oxygen into our blood, we breathe air. As shown above, in-haled air passes through the nose and mouth, down the trachea (windpipe), and into the lungs. The epiglottis, a muscle that works like a trapdoor, allows the air to enter the trachea, but closes the opening to the trachea when food or water is swallowed. Bronchial tubes branch off the trachea and carry the air into each of two lungs. In the lungs, the bronchial tubes branch into even smaller tubes that end in millions of little air sacs. It is in these tiny air sacs that blood vessels absorb the oxygen from the air. At the same time, the blood releases the waste carbon dioxide gas it has brought from the body cells.

lem? If the information is not in the article, discuss what you think they did.
- Talk about the data resulting from the exploration. What were the results?
- State the final conclusion based on the data. Why do you think it is or is not valid?
- Do you think more research should be done on the problem? If so, can you think of any questions or problems to consider for the follow-up study?

FIGURE 3.2 *Continued*

Blood, which serves the body by transporting nutrients, water, and oxygen to all body cells, is an important part of the circulatory system shown at right.

The center of the circulatory system is the heart, a fist-sized muscle that is divided into two upper chambers and two lower chambers. The upper chambers pump blood out from the heart, through the lungs, and back again to the heart. While in the lungs, the blood absorbs oxygen gas and releases waste carbon dioxide gas that it has taken from body cells. The lower chambers of the heart then pump the oxygen-rich blood from the heart and out through arteries to the rest of the body.

When it reaches body cells, the oxygen-rich blood gives up its oxygen and nutrients and picks up carbon dioxide gas. The blood, now rich in carbon dioxide, leaves the cells and returns through veins to the upper chambers of the heart. From there the carbon dioxide-rich blood begins the flow cycle once again.

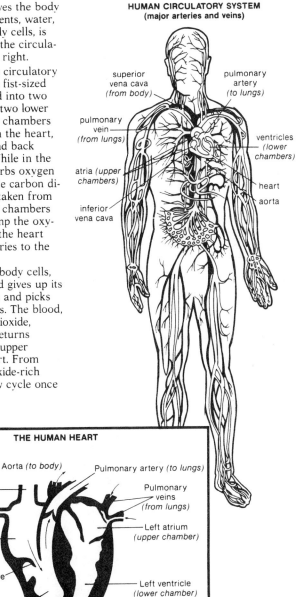

HUMAN CIRCULATORY SYSTEM
(major arteries and veins)

superior vena cava (from body)

pulmonary artery (to lungs)

pulmonary vein (from lungs)

ventricles (lower chambers)

atria (upper chambers)

heart

aorta

inferior vena cava

THE HUMAN HEART

Aorta (to body)

Pulmonary artery (to lungs)

Superior vena cava (from arms and head)

Inferior vena cava (from legs and torso)

Pulmonary veins (from lungs)

Right atrium

Left atrium (upper chamber)

Valve

Left ventricle (lower chamber)

Right ventricle

Source: Mitchell, R. (1987). *GED science.* Chicago: Contemporary Books, pp. 143–44. Used with permission

Such questions can be applied to many articles about science, such as the one from *Newsweek* in Figure 3.3.

Since the scientific method is emphasized in both GED science and social studies, another way to reinforce it is by having learners design an experiment to do in class or at home. Before they proceed with the experiment, class discussions can be conducted to help learners clearly state the problem, hypothesis, method, and conclusion. As always, a demonstration of an experiment by the teacher will be important in helping learners realize the steps and the thought processes involved as well as in motivating them to try experiments of their own. If possible, learners should design a second experiment as a control, in order to compare results and to consider the implications of generalizing from just one sample. Written guidelines such as the following might be distributed for use in preparing an experiment:

> You are a scientist interested in research. Design an experiment in an area you want to explore. List and describe the steps in your research method (identify the problem, collect information, make a hypothesis, do an experiment and record the results, draw conclusions). Have a "control" if possible.
>
> Can you think of a follow-up study? Can you think how your results might be applied to other situations?

Writing

Although writing is a separate area of the GED, various forms of writing should be incorporated in the other four areas, too. Whether in the writing class or in the other subjects, the focus is on the *process* of writing rather than on the mechanics as ends in themselves. Writings are often personal responses to a story or informational text. These purposeful writings, rather than meaningless exercises, serve as the context for learning grammar, spelling, punctuation, and capitalization.

The principles of writing instruction described in Chapter 2 are germane; suggestions will be offered for applying these principles at higher levels with GED learners. Before the writing begins, ideas are extended and enriched by class discussion. After the discussion, the teacher might suggest a purpose for writing. The purpose, always linked to the adult's experiences, might be proposed specifically to help the writer practice the variations on writing

FIGURE 3.3 Article on Scientific Study

Small Step for Mice, Large Step for Man

Build a better mousetrap and the world plops down 59 cents a shot for your discovery. But build a better mouse? That's what scientists at Harvard Medical School did, and last week the rodent became the first animal ever patented. Born with genes that promote cancer, it may become invaluable for studying the origins of that disease. But when the government granted the patent, it reignited the debate over whether man has the right both to create novel forms of life and to own them, too.

The mice produced by geneticists led by Dr. Philip Leder look as unassuming as any other laboratory rodents. They belong to a strain created when Leder's team injected, into fertilized mouse eggs, hundreds of copies of a gene that causes cancer. The mice that developed from the eggs carried the "oncogene," and passed it on to half of their offspring. Thus the technique produces a breed that spontaneously develops breast cancer. The engineered mice, licensed exclusively to Du Pont, could be used "to answer a lot of fundamental questions about cancer," says Leder, such as how genes promote tumors. They also might help screen new cancer drugs and therapies, find ways to diagnose breast cancer and test suspected carcinogens.

Opponents of the patent, which covers the creation of any oncogene-carrying mammal except man, worry about the dangers the precedent poses. Ever since the Supreme Court ruled in 1980 that bacteria could be patented, critics have assailed the idea that one animal--man--could patent and thereby own another. Although it's not obvious how that is more objectionable than, say, sending cattle to the abattoir, critics see it differently. "We are giving the private sector the right to control every form of life on this planet from apes to insect," argues Jeremy Rifkin of the anti-biotech Foundation on Economic Trends. There are more prosaic concerns, too. Because a patent guarantees a monopoly price, patenting a lab animal may increase costs of research and, ultimately, new drugs.

Congress is weighing a two-year moratorium on animal patents while it studies their ethical and economic implications. The patent office is busy studying, too: 21 applications for new animals are pending.

Source: Newsweek, April 25, 1988, p. 58, Newsweek, Inc. All rights reserved. Reprinted with permission.

style needed for description, narration, debate, or persuasion. The form of the writing might be a story, letter, essay, or poem.

Pre-writing techniques are invaluable for setting the stage for writing—for relaxing people, helping them get ideas down on paper, and providing an organizational guide. Two very useful techniques, imaging and clustering, activate the creative right brain. In imaging, the learners close their eyes and allow strong images of people, places, smells, colors, or other memories to drift through their minds. In clustering, they focus on a central idea and write around it any words that come to mind. After clustering, they develop at least one focusing statement in order to establish the central idea for the subsequent writing.

During the writing, learners should keep their focusing statements in mind so that attention is on the message first. Writing is a highly complex activity and it can be overwhelming if every aspect in both the meaning and the mechanics must be addressed at the same time. Learners must realize that the mark of good writing is communicating something well. The mechanics will help make the message clear, but a mechanically correct paper is not in and of itself good writing.

Revising (for content) and editing (for mechanics) are crucial parts of the thinking and writing process. The purpose of revision is to make the communication clear, coherent, and interesting for the intended audience. To encourage active and independent efforts, GED learners are asked to revise their own writings first, before enlisting the aid of the teacher. Similarly, editing for mechanics should be done first by the writer, then with the assistance of the teacher. During the editing, opportunities will arise for teaching or reviewing most of the elements of grammar, punctuation, spelling, and capitalization that will be part of the GED tests. Insisting that learners edit their work first helps them move toward becoming capable writers as well as learning to identify similar items on the test. Because the GED Writing Test includes an objective test of grammar, spelling, and punctuation, the teacher should set aside some time for practicing these in a multiple-choice test format as well, using examples from a textbook or an Official Practice Test. Identifying specific areas of difficulty on objective tests, discussing them, and being aware of them in writing should all contribute to a better understanding of the mechanics.

After writings have been completed, they can be collected into personal books, just as they are in reading and writing improvement classes. Adults can share their writings with others in and out of class, both to grow in self-esteem and to become better writers. In the class setting, the audience members, following the model of the teacher, will listen carefully and react positively to the content and the ideas that particularly impress them. If letters have been written, they will be sent; replies to them can also be shared with the group. If the pieces are suitable to appear in a local newspaper, the writers should be encouraged to give permission for publication.

Reading and Writing in Math

Opportunities to include discussion, reading, and writing in GED math classes should not be overlooked. Math exercises are meaningful when based on familiar experiences of learners. As in reading any text, learners should be asked to consider what they already know before beginning a lesson on a particular math concept. The illustrations used for practice of the concept should be based on situations that are encountered at work or in other areas of life. For example, actual data such as the number of parts rejected or repaired in relation to the total number of parts produced could be used when studying percentage. For an area problem in geometry, a home project involving measuring the length and width of wall to be covered with wallpaper would be realistic for many people. Discussions in math will be helpful in promoting significant learning. Math learners can discuss strategies for solving problems, the reasonableness of predictions or estimates, the appropriateness of particular math functions for a given situation, or the logic of the steps involved in calculations. It is especially beneficial for the learner to "teach" the teacher, explaining each step of a problem while solving it. Learners may also write down the steps they use, particularly if the concept is difficult to understand. After a math concept is understood, learners might create similar problems to be used with others in the class as well as to serve as examples for the teacher to use with the next group. Also, it is very useful to have students evaluate their progress orally and in writing, at least every eight weeks. The teacher should remind them to be specific about what they have learned and how it has made a positive change in their lives.

At first, learners may not understand the purpose for such activities, so the teacher should explain how discussion and writing help them learn. Although discussing and writing about math may result in fewer calculations being done, the language activities lead to deeper understandings that are more important and lasting than the practice of endless examples. Quantities of rote practice on math procedures will not make up for the quality of learning that occurs when the concept and its application to real situations are understood.

Independent Reading and Writing

Purposeful practice is imperative. While it is common to have learners practice a lot of math problems, it is not always so common to provide time to practice reading and writing. With any human activity, people develop the ability to do something well by practicing and thinking about what they are learning. To become truly independent learners, they need opportunities to practice in order to apply on their own the reading, writing, and thinking strategies that are being developed in teacher-guided lessons. They will learn best if practice is enjoyable and purposeful and if they feel successful.

One way to promote practice in reading is to have learners participate in uninterrupted sustained silent reading with material they enjoy. In GED classes, teachers might recommend books, stories, or articles related to the area the individuals are currently studying. Learners are encouraged to bring in relevant articles they find in newspapers or magazines to share with the class.

Writing, too, needs to be practiced independently of teacher-guided lessons. The GED learners should have opportunities to do unstructured "free" or journal writings in class as well as be encouraged to do so at home. In free writing, a person records for 10 minutes any observations or feelings he or she chooses. As Elbow (1973) explains, free writings help people release tension and create a flow of ideas. These writings are kept in a separate folder to be referred to later for reading and perhaps for further writing.

ILLUSTRATIVE LESSON PLANS

On the following pages, one illustrative lesson plan will be presented for each of the GED areas to show how the principles of experience-based learning can be implemented.

Literature and the Arts

The teacher has much flexibility in creating lessons for Literature and the Arts (Romanek, 1987). The example given here is one way of helping learners appreciate rich description in reading and incorporate it into their writing.

Lesson Objectives. In this lesson, learners will

- visualize a scene described in nonfiction prose
- describe what they could see, hear, and touch
- explain the effect of descriptive words in writing
- write a description of a place, using appropriate descriptive words

Preparation. Using a descriptive passage from a textbook or other source (see Figure 3.4), the teacher will prepare an abridged version by removing most of the descriptive words (as in Figure 3.5). Sharp pencils, blank paper, and lined paper should be available.

Procedure. Explain that two versions of a description will be read for the purpose of visualizing the material. Distribute the abridged version and have the learners read the title and the author's name. Ask, "What do you think the passage will be about?" After the first sentence has been read, ask questions such as: "Has anyone been to Oklahoma or other states in that area? What kind of weather would you expect to find there? What might you see on a plain?" Now have the learners read the passage silently, suggesting that they form pictures in their minds as they read. You might say, "Imagine you are walking with Momaday on the plain in Oklahoma, looking at Rainy Mountain and the surrounding landscape." After they finished reading ask, "What image did you have of the landscape? What can you tell about Momaday and how he feels about that part of the world?"

Have the learners read the original version. Suggest that they concentrate on what they now see, hear, touch, or feel as they imagine walking around. After they have finished reading, guide them to think vividly of the details by discussing the following: "Did anything you read surprise you? What did you see? What could you hear? What did you feel?" Have them compare the two versions in

FIGURE 3.4   Original Version of Excerpt
for Literature and Arts Lesson

The Way to Rainy Mountain

A single knoll rises out of the plain in Oklahoma, north and west of the Wichita range. For my people, the Kiowas, it is an old landmark, and they gave it the name Rainy Mountain. The hardest weather in the world is there. Winter brings blizzards, hot tornadic winds arise in the spring, and in the summer the prairie is an anvil's edge. The grass turns brittle and brown, and it cracks beneath your feet. There are green belts along the rivers and creeks, linear groves of hickory and pecan, willow and witch hazel. At a distance in July or August the steaming foliage seems almost to writhe in fire. Great green and yellow grasshoppers are everywhere in the tall grass, popping up like corn to sting the flesh, and tortoises crawl about on the red earth, going nowhere in the plenty of time. Loneliness is an aspect of the land. All things in the plain are isolate; there is no confusion of objects in the eye, but one hill or one tree or one man. To look upon that landscape in the early morning, with the sun at your back, is to lose the sense of proportion. Your imagination comes to life, and this, you think, is where Creation was begun.

Source: Momaday, N. S. (1969). *The way to rainy mountain.* Albuquerque, NM: The University of New Mexico Press. Reprinted in Romanek, E. (1987). *GED Literature and the Arts.* Chicago: Contemporary Books, p. 103. Used with permission of The University of New Mexico Press and Contemporary Books.

---

terms of the pictures they were able to create in their minds and then have them give reasons why the original version was more stimulating.

Now provide time for class members to picture a place they enjoy. Prompt them as follows: "Take a deep breath. Close your eyes. Let images of places drift through your mind. When an image begins to form, let it develop and grow stronger." When they appear ready, tell them, "Begin to cluster around the name of that place. Use as many descriptive words as possible. When you are done clustering, write a focusing statement—one sentence to show what main idea you will be writing about. Then begin writing. Concentrate on your ideas; don't worry about spelling at this point. You

FIGURE 3.5 Abridged Version of Excerpt
for Literature and Arts Lesson

The Way to Rainy Mountain

A single knoll rises out of the plain in Oklahoma. For my people, the Kiowas, it is an old landmark, and they gave it the name Rainy Mountain. The hardest weather in the world is there. . . . Loneliness is an aspect of the land. . . . To look upon that landscape in the early morning, with the sun at your back, is to lose the sense of proportion. Your imagination comes to life, and this, you think, is where Creation was begun.

Source: Momaday, N. S. (1969). *The way to rainy mountain.* Albuquerque, NM: The University of New Mexico Press. Reprinted in Romanek, E. (1987). *GED Literature and the Arts.* Chicago: Contemporary Books, p. 103. Used with permission of The University of New Mexico Press and Contemporary Books.

don't have to use all the words in your cluster, and of course you should let other descriptive words flow out as images come to mind while you're writing." Observe the learners and help those who are having difficulty getting started by sitting with them, talking about places they have seen, and, if necessary, clustering with them.

As individuals finish writing, remind them to read over what has been written and make changes as needed. Sit with them when they are ready to enlist your aid in revising and editing. Your role during the revising is to react first to the ideas, being sure to find something to praise as well as possibly finding changes to suggest. During the next phase, editing, you can point out places where corrections are needed, guiding learners to make the changes whenever they are able. In providing guidance rather than authoritative corrections, you could say something like, "This sentence is standing alone. You could add a sentence to expand that idea, combine it with another paragraph, or erase it." Give the person a reasonable time to think and respond. The learner is usually able to select the best option for handling an orphaned sentence. The teacher should make a suggestion for revision only if the person needs clarification. In later lessons, you might simply say, "What are some things that can be done with this one sentence that seems to stand by itself?" For spelling you might indicate the misspelled word and say, "A letter is missing here. What are some possibilities for that sound?" For tense, "This is written in the past. What ending should go here?" As the time for the end of class nears and some individuals are still writing or you haven't been able to confer with them, make a point of responding at least briefly to their content and having them plan to complete the writing during the next class.

Two copies of the finished writings should be typed. One will be put into the learners' personal books and the other will be rewritten as explained in Chapter 2. Writings should be shared, and in doing so with this particular lesson, emphasis should be on having listeners visualize the place described and giving positive comments to the author about the descriptive words that helped create a good image.

Social Studies

The following lesson is to be used in conjunction with textbook material on the three branches of the government of the United States (Digilio, 1987, pp. 149–153). Attention is given to the social studies content of the lesson as well as reading and writing strategies. The suggested writing is a letter to members of Congress or the President.

Lesson Objectives.   In this lesson, learners will

- organize information regarding the legislative, executive, and judicial branches of the government
- describe the involvement of each of the branches in relation to the development and implementation of a law
- compare news articles and editorials about a recent law or ruling
- express an opinion about a law or ruling in the form of a letter to a member of Congress or the President

Preparation.   A pre-reading activity for the textbook material should be planned. For this lesson, the names of the three branches of the government and words associated with them can be written randomly on the board, as shown in Figure 3.6. In addition, newspaper and magazine articles about recent laws passed by Congress, presidential signings or vetoes, and Supreme Court rulings should be gathered. An editorial on a current congressional

FIGURE 3.6   Random Terms for Social Studies Lesson

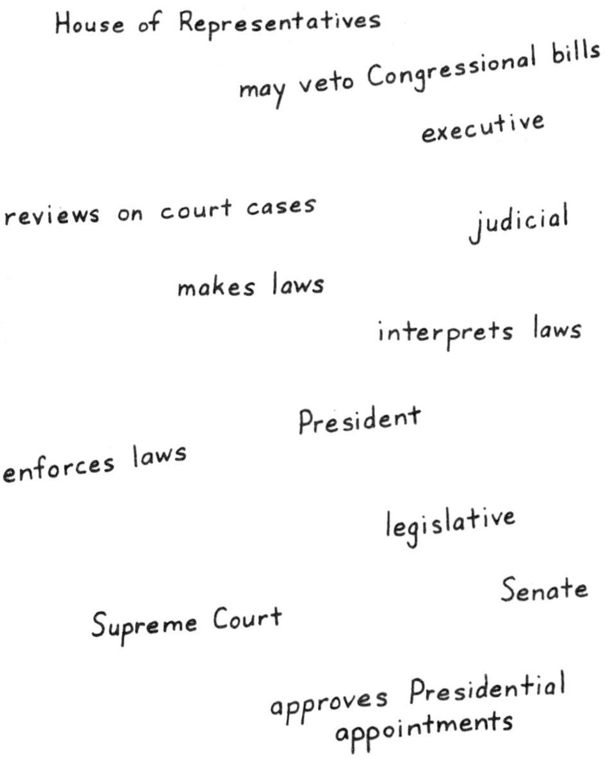

House of Representatives

may veto Congressional bills

executive

reviews on court cases   judicial

makes laws

interprets laws

President

enforces laws

legislative

Senate

Supreme Court

approves Presidential
appointments

bill will be needed, such as the one in Figure 3.7. Learners will need their social studies textbooks, a copy of the editorial, the names and addresses of their representatives or senators and the President, sharp pencils, markers, blank paper, and lined paper.

Procedure.   Using the randomly placed terms and phrases on the board (Figure 3.6), learners can work in pairs to group them into categories. When they have finished, they can tell how they organized the words. This procedure will alert them to the fact that information about the government might be organized in a similar way in a text, that is, by identifying the people who work in each branch and describing the powers they have. With their background knowledge thus activated, learners can read the related section of the textbook, seeking to confirm and evaluate the infor-

FIGURE 3.7   An Editorial for a Social Studies Lesson

PLANT CLOSINGS:
Advance notice for workers is simple fairness

More than 400,000 Americans--a figure nearly equal to the total number of people who work in Detroit--lost their jobs last year because of plant closing or other mass layoffs. Two out of three workers get no advance warning of layoffs from their employers, according to a U. S. Department of Labor study. Expecting large companies to give prior notice of factory shutdowns or large-scale layoffs seems a matter of basic fairness to workers, families and communities who face the enormous upheaval such job losses bring. That's why we support a bill adopted by the U. S. Senate last week, requiring 60 days' notice of plant closings, despite the difficulties it may create for some troubled businesses.

Under the Senate bill, all employers of more than 100 workers must give advance written notice--to employes and local government officials--of any closing affecting at least one-third of a plant's workers or causing the permanent layoffs of 50 or more full-time employes. Business interests oppose the measure as an improper government encroachment on private-sector decisions. They argue that public exposure of a plant's imminent shutdown could jeopardize its relations with suppliers, creditors and customers, and make it more difficult to sell the factory to a new owner. The net result, they contend, would be business failures and a greater loss of jobs.

We acknowledge that the plant-closing bill could rob faltering companies of some flexibility in their attempts to remain competitive and survive by restructuring themselves. It could subject them to increased litigation. Business conditions can change enormously in 60 days or far fewer, as last year's stock market crash demonstrated. Yet we still think these potential drawbacks are outweighed by the humane considerations involved in allowing dislocated workers more time and opportunity to prepare for new jobs and rebuild their lives.

The Senate bill does exempt companies trying to raise capital to keep a plant open, if the notice requirement disrupts that effort. It also does not cover layoffs caused by a natural disaster or other unpredictable circumstances and does not apply when workers are on strike. Suggestions that many major employers, such as General Motors Corp., already provide advance word voluntarily of major plant closings make a more compelling argument for mandatory notice provisions that would cover less responsible companies as well. Indeed, unions initially demanded a 180-day notice requirement.

The wide margin by which the bill passed the Senate, after GOP attempts to water it down and delay it failed, suggests it could survive a threatened veto by President Ronald Reagan if the House also approves the measure as expected this week. But even if Mr. Reagan opposes the legislation on ideological grounds, its overwhelming public popularity--as measured by opinion polls-- suggests the political dangers of a veto, to the president and his party, months before a national election.

When Mr. Reagan vetoed an omnibus trade bill Congress had sent him in May, he cited its plant closing language--virtually identical to the Senate measure adopted last week--as his chief objection. He had good reasons to reject the trade bill, especially its protectionist aspects, but the advance-notice provision wasn't one of them. On balance, by itself, the provision would be good, compassionate law.

Source: The Detroit Free Press, July 8, 1988, p. 12A. Used with permission.

mation that has been organized. After reading, they can make any necessary changes to their organization of the phrases.

They can then proceed to further discussion about the branches of the government, considering such questions as: "Why did the writers of the Constitution establish a separation of powers? What new information did you get about the legislative branch? The executive branch? The judicial branch?" To apply these concepts to today's world, learners might be asked to recall any recent bills that have been passed, vetoed by the President, or reviewed by the Supreme Court. Pertinent newspaper and magazine articles can be skimmed for confirmations of and additions to their knowledge about such events. Many times this type of activity will spur adults to be on the lookout for other articles to bring to future classes.

Attention can now be turned from the factual information about new laws to an editorial about a recent congressional bill, such as shown in Figure 3.7. After the learners read the title, "Plant Closings: Advance notice for workers is simple fairness," ask them if they are aware of the bill that is involved and, if so, what opinions they have about the matter. They might consider whether everyone would have the same opinion, who might hold different views and why, and what opinion might be reflected by the local newspaper editorial staff. They should now be ready to read the editorial silently, looking for both the factual information that a good editor should include and the point of view expressed. In the subsequent discussion, they could compare the way in which news articles about the bill differ from editorials about it. They might further consider how they think their senators and representatives would (or did) vote on the issue.

The stage is set for writing a letter to one of their representatives in Congress or to the President about the issue. To organize ideas to support their opinions, the clustering technique can be used. Each of the supporting ideas on the cluster can be written as a main idea and then elaborated as the letter is composed. Following the revising, editing, and sharing with fellow class members, duplicate copies of the letters can be made. The originals, of course, should be mailed.

Science

In this lesson on the greenhouse effect, a cartoon is used as the pre-reading stimulus. Textbook material and an illustrated magazine article are used to provide science information and practice in applying reading strategies to content area texts. The related writing assignment is an essay.

Lesson Objectives.   In this lesson, learners will

- interpret information and point of view presented in cartoon fashion
- use textual aids to predict the organization and content of printed material
- organize information to indicate cause–effect relationships
- explain the purpose and values of graphic aids
- write a persuasive essay

Preparation.   The stimulus for the pre-reading activity might be a political cartoon from a newspaper (Figure 3.8). Textbook information (Figure 3.9) and magazine articles on the topic are also available. Sharp pencils, colored markers, blank paper, and lined paper will be needed for the writing.

Procedure.   As the cartoon is viewed, elicit comments about the greenhouse effect by asking such questions as, "How do you feel

FIGURE 3.8 Newspaper Cartoon on the Greenhouse Effect

THE GREENHOUSE EFFECT

Source: The Detroit Free Press, July 8, 1988, p. 10A. Used with permission.

when you are in a greenhouse on a hot day? How can the whole earth become a greenhouse? What is happening to the earth? How does the cartoon help explain the greenhouse effect? What do you think is getting trapped in the earth's greenhouse?" Before reading the text, learners can think about possible causes for the greenhouse effect. Write the word "Causes" on the board and list their responses. Also in preparation for reading, compare and contrast the two graphics shown in the text (Figure 3.9) and determine what additional information they give about the causes. Have the learners read the subheading, "Consequences of the Greenhouse Effect," and make predictions about the content of that section. List their ideas on another section of the board under the word "Consequences." After they read the text material, the lists of "Causes" and "Consequences" should be reviewed and changes or additions made to them.

Magazine articles can be distributed as additional sources of

FIGURE 3.9 Text for Science Lesson on the Greenhouse Effect

The Greenhouse Effect

Key Word

greenhouse effect—a warming of the Earth's atmosphere as a result of pollution

---

Life on Earth is made possible by a delicate balance of many biological and chemical factors. If this balance is upset, the results can be disastrous. You already know how the disposal of garbage can affect the lives of many land and marine animals. In this section, we'll discuss how another form of pollution can affect all life on Earth simply by causing a slow increase in the temperature of our planet.

Our close neighbor, the planet Venus, has experienced such a temperature increase. Because it is the closest planet to the Earth and appears to be made up of the same minerals, you might think that Venus is a place where living organisms could develop and grow. Not so. In fact, the surface temperature of Venus is about 900°F—so hot that no form of life could hope to exist there.

The reason that Venus is so hot is that its atmosphere contains a large amount of carbon dioxide. Because of this gas, Venus can't cool the way other planets cool, by sending heat energy back out into space. Instead, the heat energy is absorbed by the carbon dioxide.

This natural heating of the atmosphere of Venus is commonly called the greenhouse effect. The greenhouse effect gets its name from the glass-sided and glass-roofed buildings that you see in plant nurseries. In a nursery greenhouse, sunlight freely passes though the glass and warms the soil, plants, and air inside. The glass prevents the heat from leaving. The result is that the greenhouse stays warm enough for plant growth even though the temperature outside may be below freezing. On Venus, the dense carbon dioxide atmosphere traps heat and keeps surface heat energy from escaping back into space. Unfortunately, unlike a real greenhouse, the high temperature on Venus can't be controlled simply by opening a few windows!

FIGURE 3.9 *Continued*

On Earth, the current level of carbon dioxide gas in the atmosphere keeps the Earth's temperature in the range it is in now. However, the burning of wood, coal, oil, and other hydrocarbons is adding an abnormal amount of carbon dioxide to the atmosphere. The result is that the level of this gas has been slowly increasing since at least 1958, when scientists started to follow carefully atmospheric levels of carbon dioxide. The Earth's temperature has been gradually going up as well. Most probably, the increases have taken place since the beginning of the Industrial Revolution in the late eighteenth century.

CONSTANT CO$_2$ IN ATMOSPHERE

With a constant level of carbon dioxide in the atmosphere, the Earth cools by radiating excess heat back into space.

INCREASED CO$_2$ IN ATMOSPHERE

As the high level of carbon dioxide in the atmosphere increases, the Earth's average temperature also increases.

Consequences of the Greenhouse Effect

No one is sure just what the consequences of the greenhouse effect will be in the long run. However, many scientists feel that, if the addition of carbon dioxide to the atmosphere continues unchecked, several things could eventually happen:

- The average surface temperature of the Earth will increase, perhaps by as much as 6°F to 10°F in the next fifty years.

- The warming effect will cause a lot of glacial ice to melt. This will result in the oceans rising by a couple of feet during the same fifty years. Over a period of a couple of hundred years, ocean levels could rise by as much as twenty or more feet. Cities like San Francisco and New York would find themselves under water!

- A rising surface temperature will also probably change world rainfall patterns. The United States, now the breadbasket of the world, could become an arid, parched wasteland.

Though no one is sure just how serious these effects may be and how soon they may occur, one thing is certain: all the countries on Earth live together under a single shared atmosphere. People are now coming to see that proper care of this atmosphere is a must if the Earth's environment is to remain capable of sustaining human life.

Source: Mitchell, R. (1987). *GED science.* Chicago: Contemporary Books, Inc., pp. 217–218. Used with permission.

information. The learners should be encouraged to glean as much information as possible from the titles, pictures, and captions. They might look for indications of whether the articles are organized in a cause–effect pattern. Then they can skim the materials to find additional causes or consequences of the greenhouse effect and compare the information provided in the different sources. For this particular topic, articles in the July 11, 1988 issue of *Newsweek* (pp. 16–23) would be invaluable, not only for the content but also for a wealth of illustrations and graphics that learners could interpret.

To apply this information to their own lives, the learners might be asked to write an essay about ways in which individuals can reduce the greenhouse effect. They might develop a cluster of ideas, write a brief outline, and then write an essay to persuade others to take steps to help alleviate the situation. After revision and editing, some of the essays might be deemed appropriate for submission to a local newspaper or an in-house publication.

Mathematics

The following lesson on finding the part in percent problems is a segment of a larger lesson on finding the part, percent, or whole (Howett, 1987). Textbook exercises are combined with job-related problems created by previous learners. Current learners will, in turn, write problems for succeeding groups.

Lesson Objectives. In this lesson, learners will

- relate uses of percents to personal experiences
- use the concept of proportion as the basis for determining percent, part, and whole
- apply principles of percents to textbook problems
- apply principles of percents to prepared job-related math problems
- create job-related math problems involving percents

Preparation. In addition to the math textbook, learners will need paper and sharp pencils. If possible, the teacher should have available job-related problems created by adults in previous classes.

Procedure. The concept of percent might be introduced by guiding learners to relate it to "cents." Not all adults have connected percentage to the fact that there are 100 cents in a dollar. This fact is background knowledge that should help people understand that percents are expressed as part of a base of 100. To relate this concept to their own circumstances, they can consider how much money a 15 percent tip would be for a restaurant bill of $5.15. If help is needed, the teacher might think aloud one way to figure this out, saying, "I first figure how much I would leave for $1.00 (15 cents for each dollar). I then round the $5.15 bill to the nearest dollar and think how much I will leave for $5.00 ($.15 times 5 equals 75 cents)."

In solving written math problems, the first step is to determine what is given and what is asked for. Relating this to percent problems, the teacher can explain that either the percent, the part, or the whole must be found. Recalling the tipping situation, learners can be guided to verbalize that the percent is given and is often indicated by the % symbol. The figure that must be found is the part, that is, the part of the total to leave as a tip. As these points are being brought out, the following proportion can be written on the board:

$$\frac{part}{whole} = \frac{\%}{100}$$

$$\frac{part}{\$5} = \frac{15}{100}$$

Now the teacher can demonstrate how the problem is solved, saying, "Look for two numbers to cross-multiply, then divide by the one that's left." Write the equation "15 × $5 = $75" on the board and remind learners that the $75 must be divided by 100. If they remember earlier lessons, they will realize that the shortcut for division by 100 is to move the hidden decimal point two spaces to the left, that is, $75. divided by 100 = $.75. The long division method of changing a fraction to a decimal can also be reviewed at this time and the procedure shown on the board to provide reinforcement for learners who might understand the concept better one way than the other or who might be helped to see one more time why the shortcut of moving the decimal point works.

At this time, learners might apply this procedure to the examples in the textbook. The teacher should circulate and ask people how they are doing, thus involving them in assessing their own understanding of the concept. They should also be asked to explain the method they are using—not for the teacher to see if they know, but rather for them to verbalize and therefore reinforce their understanding of the procedure.

Job-related problems by fellow learners and co-workers can provide additional practice, such as the three examples that follow.

1. Carl has two machines that weld brackets. The production for his department is 250/hour for each machine. At that rate, the machines would produce 4,250 parts in an 8-hour day. What percent of 4,250 is 250?
2. Ginny and her co-workers had to band 48 gray racks containing 6,048 shocks. They were able to band 25% of the shocks in about two hours. How many did they band in those two hours?
3. Larry pressed about 240 parts on Monday. This was 15% of his weekly output. How many parts did he press that week?

As each new example is approached, the solver should first note orally, if not in writing, whether he or she is looking for the part, the percent, or the whole.

When learners have completed the examples created by others, they should create some of their own. The intent is not to provide teaching materials for future lessons (although that will be one of the outcomes), but rather to add to the learner's understanding of the math concepts involved. In the pre-writing stage, the teacher should talk with the learners about their jobs and elicit data that can be used in a percentage problem. To guide the writing of problems, interaction between the teacher and learner such as outlined in Figure 3.10 is helpful.

Writing

The GED learners should be "in on the secret" of how writing is evaluated. In this lesson, they will become familiar with the process of holistic scoring, which will help them evaluate their own writings. They will also realize how the clustering technique can contribute to better organized papers that will result in higher assessments.

Lesson Objectives. In this lesson, learners will

- describe the concept of holistic scoring of essays
- use the Guidelines for Scoring the GED Essay Test to rate sample essays

FIGURE 3.10   Creating a Job-Related Percent Problem

The teacher can ask the learner to provide actual job data suitable for a percent problem, then create the problem. The problem can then be used to review rounding, fractions, and decimals.

Q: What do you do in your job?

A: I make field coils.

Q: What is your production goal?

A: 2,750 field coils.

Q: How much did you produce in one day?

A: 400.

Q: What percent do you have to complete? The learner may need review questioning to arrive at the problem.

Q: Can you think of how to set up the percent problem as a proportion?

A: $\dfrac{400}{2,750} \Big| \dfrac{\%}{100}$

Q: That's right for the percent produced. How could you set up a proportion for the percent you have to complete?

A: $\begin{array}{r} 2,750 \\ -\ 400 \\ \hline 2,350 \end{array}$ $\dfrac{2,350}{2,750} \Big| \dfrac{\%}{100}$

Q: Great! Now, can you write the problem? (Facilitate if necessary with additional questions.)

A: Marianne has to make 2,750 field coils. She already produced 400. What percent does she have to complete?

Q: Fine. You can add, "Round to the nearest hundredth." (Have the learner work out the problem.) If you have 85% to complete, what fraction would that be?

A: $\dfrac{85}{100} = \dfrac{17}{20}$

Q: Very good. How did you feel about doing this activity? How did it help your understanding of percent?

- compare their ratings with the official scores and determine reasons for differences
- evaluate personal essays, using the guidelines

Preparation.   The Guidelines for Scoring the GED Essay Test and sample handwritten essays (such as those in *The 1988 Tests of*

General Educational Development: A Preview, GED Testing Service, 1985), sharp pencils, blank paper, and lined paper should be available.

Procedure. Show learners the Guidelines for Scoring the GED Essay Test and prepare them to take the role of judges of essays. Talk about the meaning of "holistic" scoring, in which an essay is evaluated based on the writer's ability to state and support ideas about a given topic. Explain that when the actual GED essays are judged, two raters must come to a consensus on a score. While the raters consider major problems in spelling, capitalization, and punctuation, these are secondary to the content. The raters understand that they are reading a first draft, so it isn't necessary that a paper be mechanically perfect to receive even the highest score of six points. After the GED learners read the scoring guidelines briefly, they are told that the first step in rating a paper is to decide if it falls in the upper or lower half. They might talk to one another about the distinction between upper-half and lower-half papers, and then think about what is taken into consideration in breaking those ratings down to the finer six-point scale.

These insights about rating can now be applied to sample essays that have been officially scored. Samples of these are available from the GED Testing Service (1985). Working in pairs, the learners must agree on a score for each essay, then compare their score with the official rating. If their scores are different, they should look again at the guidelines to see why the official raters probably assigned a certain score.

The teacher might now demonstrate how clustering and outlining before writing on a given topic will make any writing easier and more coherent, and furthermore will help learners meet the criteria for the writing portion of the GED test. The following topic suggested by Wickham (1987) might serve as the model: "Debates about the effects of television on children have raged for years. In particular, some groups have suggested that commercials be banned from children's programs. Describe some effects that television commercials can have on children" (p. 283). Learners must realize that they will have only 45 minutes to plan, write, and proof their essays. This suggests a simple cluster, in which ideas are listed, uncircled, under main topics. Using a cluster rather than a list, writers can brainstorm quickly but still see the relationships between ideas. The teacher might model the preparation of a cluster (as shown in Figure 3.11) and an outline derived from that cluster, such as the following:

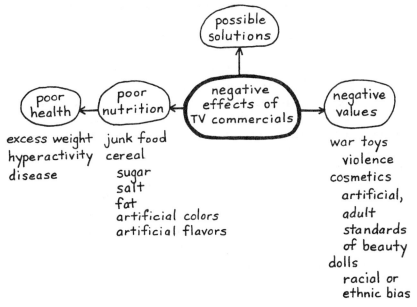

parents educate children to think about products
TV stations balance with educational commercials
government monitors content

FIGURE 3.11 Cluster for Essay on TV Commercials

OUTLINE FOR ESSAY ON TV COMMERCIALS

Paragraph 1: Introduction—TV commercials can have a negative effect on children (values, nutrition)

Paragraph 2: Development—Watching commercials can promote violence, artificial adult standards of beauty, and ethnic bias

Paragraph 3: Development—Children are urged to eat products high in sugar, salt, and fat

Paragraph 4: Conclusion—TV commercials could seriously affect our children's future and thus the future of society

Having seen the model, learners might now write an essay of their own, using clustering and outlining, to which they can later apply the scoring guidelines. For their first essay, they can use the same topic as that given for the sample essays they rated, if they wish; since the first attempt at an essay may be threatening, the topic should be one with which they are familiar. The teacher should observe the writing, and the teacher and learner together should consider whether additional help on clustering or writing outlines is needed. Writers should be encouraged to draw on their personal experiences as much as possible, even though they will be writing in the impersonal essay style. The revising and editing procedure described in the lesson for Literature and the Arts should be followed, with emphasis on doing this independently, as it must be done during the actual test situation.

As a follow-up to the writing, learners might work together or with the teacher to apply the guidelines to their essays. Since they followed a clustering procedure, the results should be positive and should be an important step toward building the confidence needed for the formal test.

In subsequent classes, learners should be given many opportunities to write papers on a variety of topics. These might be selected from their writing, science, and social studies textbooks or from newspapers and magazines. Such writing will enhance general knowledge of content as well as provide practice in the process of writing essays.

SUMMARY: GED—AND BEYOND

Although the tangible outcome of successful GED instruction is the passing of the tests by the learner, the intangible outcomes from the type of instruction described in this chapter are even more important. Suggestions are offered for each of the GED areas—Literature and the Arts, Social Studies, Science, Mathematics, and Writing—to foster the acquisition of attitudes and learning strategies that go far beyond merely retaining information to pass tests. Whole language activities—discussion, writing, and reading—help learners connect their wealth of experiences with subject matter and thus ensure that they learn both the content and, more important, the processes that will enable them to continue as lifelong learners.

How exciting for an adult to receive a GED certificate! Accomplishing this goal often means as much or more to an adult than receiving a high school diploma means to a teenager. The teacher who works alongside an adult during his or her progress toward the goal is equally rewarded. Both the learner and the teacher gain renewed excitement about learning. Even more significant, an individual sees himself or herself as an important member of society and realizes an enhanced sense of self-fulfillment.

« 4 »

Getting Comfortable
With Computers

Adults feel a need to become familiar with the technology that is a part of society today. Some people want to become confident in approaching new tools in their work environments, some wish to have a better understanding of what their children are doing with computers in schools, and some are simply curious about the "new machines." Whatever the reason, adults seek an introductory course that will help them

- understand the terminology
- feel comfortable and confident with technology
- know what the capabilities of computers are

Because specific understandings and skills are needed to use a computer competently and confidently, a training program in which the emphasis is on rather formal presentation of information and rote practice of operational steps might seem necessary. This need not be the case, however; an effective computer awareness course can be developed in which the emphasis is on learners and the process of learning. The information and operations can be acquired as adults participate in lessons in which concepts and practice activities are related to background knowledge and familiar experiences. The environment for these lessons can be one in which dynamic interactions occur. Adults can be guided to learn how to learn about operating equipment and using software programs, rather than follow a series of directions that they attempt to commit to memory. They can engage in group discussions in which they relate prior experiences to the topics being studied and reinforce their learning by verbalizing about concepts, procedures, discoveries, and feelings.

These principles have implications for both the content and

the instructional procedures for a computer course. A practical hands-on course, with an emphasis on how and why to use computers rather than on the internal mechanics and programming languages, is suggested. The computer awareness course described in this chapter focuses on four types of application programs: word processors, databases, graphs, and spreadsheets. By using each application program in a meaningful way, adults learn its features and values and, at the same time, gain confidence in using the hardware and manipulating the disks. Attention is centered on the general concept of each type of program, for example, understanding the functions of a database rather than learning all the intricacies of a particular database package. In addition to the four major application programs, learners should have hands-on experiences with other menu-driven programs and an opportunity to try computers other than the brand used for the major part of the instruction. Well-planned experiences of this type will help learners realize not only that they must but that they can transfer their knowledge to new situations. Guided activities with programming can be provided toward the end of the course, when they will make some sense. Explanations of the functions of disk operating systems, such as formatting disks for word processing files, will be embedded in the lessons when needed.

A course consisting of 16 sessions is recommended. Classes might meet twice weekly for one and one-half hours over a period of eight weeks, giving each participant three hours of instruction and guided practice a week, for a total of twenty-four hours. Meeting twice a week provides regular spaced practice without overly long sessions and without a whole week intervening between classes. Another reason for a twice-a-week schedule is that working adults with family responsibilities are often more willing to commit themselves to eight weeks than to sixteen weeks for a course. Obviously, the sessions could also be spread over a semester or term, if the course must fit within such a schedule.

In this chapter, objectives and an overview of content for a computer awareness course are presented. Some general guidelines for the format of class sessions are provided next. Because of the variety of content and activities, each lesson will have unique features; therefore, three illustrative lessons are described to show how the general guidelines can be translated into action and adapted to fit the topic for the day. The chapter concludes with brief comments about matters of class size, open lab time, selection of software, and learner-created materials.

Before we turn to the specifics of a course, however, issues about reading levels must be addressed. Is there a minimum reading ability required for success in learning to use computers? How can teachers handle the range of differences in reading abilities in a computer awareness course?

READING ISSUES

Obviously, computer users must have some reading abilities in order to interpret menus and follow directions on software programs. Adults in many different circumstances with varied reading proficiencies will be interested in learning about computers. Attention must be given to the range of reading abilities that enrollees might have. Decisions must be made as to whether a particular degree of proficiency is required for entry to the class. This decision will be based to a large extent on the sensitivity of teachers to the participants' abilities and on their willingness to adapt teaching styles to the inevitable differences. Perhaps it is more important that the teacher be familiar with reading and writing processes and proficient in incorporating related strategies in computer classes than that a level of reading competency for adult learners in the class be specified.

Assuming that the teachers are sensitive and are willing and able to adapt the instruction, the best means of determining eligibility for a course is the learner's motivation. If an adult wants to take a computer course, that should be the main criterion. Adults do not deliberately set themselves up for failure; if they are concerned about their ability to handle the reading aspects, they will not elect the course. If learners feel they are able to meet the reading demands, the teacher must observe and use a variety of strategies to build upon the range of abilities found in any group.

Indications of abilities can be gathered by thoughtful observation as learners engage in activities requiring reading. If an introductory questionnaire is used, some indications of reading proficiency might be noted from learners' responses to it. Suggestions for ways to alleviate anxieties caused by such a questionnaire are included in the illustrative plan for a "getting started" lesson. The alert teacher will also get indications of learners' abilities as they read menus for introductory software programs.

Picking up on observations, the teacher can try several techniques to see what type of assistance is most helpful. If the learner seems lost in the midst of using a software program, the teacher can ask what he or she is trying to do and encourage the person to examine the screen for clues as to how to proceed. If that strategy brings no response, the teacher can read aloud the items on the menu, asking which of the items matches the situation. A learner who still seems unsure can be asked to verbalize the task; the teacher can then read aloud while pointing to the words on the screen, encouraging the person to decide which of the terms fits the task. Over a period of time, learners with limited reading abilities will begin to recognize key words on their own, especially since the menus on software programs tend to use a lot of similar terms.

The technique just outlined for helping with reading is the same as that used in facilitating the learning of content for all learners during practice sessions. The teacher's role during hands-on practice is to be available, as needs arise, to model the thinking process or to ask questions that will encourage learners to explore. The teacher must be continually aware of each adult's involvement with the lesson and level of comfort. Knowing *when* to intervene is extremely important; knowing *how* to intervene is even more important. When learners have a question, they will become independent through an approach in which they are guided to identify the problem, explore the options, and draw a conclusion. To promote independent learning and transfer to other situations, a guided discovery approach is more valuable to the learner than having a specific answer provided.

Learners can get reading help not only from the teacher but from each other. Many class members will apply the helping strategies modeled by the teacher—which means a consistent model must be provided. Some people will need to be reminded that the most effective way of assisting another is to guide him or her to think through the ways in which the words on the screen will help. Because many learners have had years of experience with "teaching as telling," the teacher may occasionally find it necessary to remind individuals or the group about ways of helping without giving the answer. When assistance is provided, the final decision is made and action is taken by the learner; the one who is requesting help should always be the one who physically carries out the task, that is, presses the keys, changes the disk, or otherwise resolves the problem. Whether assistance is provided by the teacher or by another learner, the helper must keep hands off the computer.

Actually the best way to learn is to teach someone else. When learners assist each other, the one being helped may figure out how to resolve a problem, while at the same time the helper reinforces his or her learning; one gets help with reading, while the other strengthens his or her understanding of the concept. An effective way to deal with differences in reading ability, therefore, is to create a cooperative learning environment, making sure that the learners are aware of the benefits of working together. Indeed, because of these benefits, some activities might be planned specifically for teams of learners to work on together, even if each person has a computer on which to work. Although techniques might be used with the covert objective of assisting with reading, the overt focus will be on learning about computers.

As will be evident from these comments, the effective computer teacher must have competencies beyond knowledge of hardware and software if the course is going to serve the many adults with varied reading abilities who will need and want to use technology in today's world. Although it may seem like an ideal, it does seem more humane and beneficial to a technological society to prepare a computer teacher to deal with a range of abilities than to eliminate numbers of learners because they do not perform at a specified reading level.

OBJECTIVES FOR A COMPUTER AWARENESS COURSE

An effective way of helping learners become comfortable with computers is to have them use programs with which they can accomplish meaningful tasks. Most people readily understand the uses of word processors for writing letters and reports. Even though they may not know the term "database," they quickly realize that many types of information in society today, including their own address books, are compiled as databases that are easily searched and sorted. Budgeting and record-keeping functions are of interest to most adults, so the transfer of these concepts to the use of spreadsheets makes sense to them. Graphs are commonly used in printed materials and are important in many work settings; thus graphing programs will be meaningful. Through using these four application programs, then, learners will develop, in a functional way, many concepts about using computers and managing files and disks.

Upon the successful completion of a computer awareness course designed around these application programs, therefore, the learner will be able to:

- Read and follow instructions on menu-driven programs
- Understand the concepts of word processing, database, spreadsheets, and graphing programs
- Enter, revise, edit, and print text with a word processor
- Enter data, search, design, and print a database
- Enter data, calculate, design, and print a spreadsheet application
- Create, edit, and print bar, line, and pie graphs
- Perform disk management operations
- Distinguish between the two types of computer memory: RAM and ROM
- Explain the purpose of programming
- Describe the functions and uses of computers in society and the workplace
- Make wise decisions about purchases of software and hardware.

COURSE OVERVIEW

The following overview suggests possible content for a computer awareness course of 16 sessions. Lessons should be designed on the principle that each topic is initiated with firsthand experiences, while explanations of concepts and terminology are incorporated as integral parts of the lesson. For example, concepts about the purpose and values of word processing will evolve as activities are carried out rather than be explained in an abstract manner as the first step in the lesson. A 16-session computer awareness course might include the following components:

1. The beginning session (or two) is spent learning to boot a disk and run menu-driven programs to make signs or posters. (Suggestions for a session on getting started with computers are presented later in this chapter.)
2. Learners use the main functions and features of word processing and spelling checkers to write and edit personal letters, compose newspaper articles, and write comments about the course as evaluative feedback to the teacher. (A sample introductory word processing lesson is described later in the chapter.) Suggested time: four sessions.
3. The purpose and format of databases are introduced as learners search prepared databases on topics such as television, automobiles, local points of interest, and sports (see Figure 4.1) and

FIGURE 4.1 A Database Form on Sports

LAST NAME: FIRST NAME:

SEX (M OR F):   CLASS #:

FAVORITE SPORT TO WATCH:

FAVORITE TEAM:

FAVORITE PLAYER (THIS YEAR):

FAVORITE ALL-TIME PLAYER:

FAVORITE SPORT TO PLAY:

FAVORITE WATER SPORT:

HOURS OF SPORTS WATCHED ON TV EACH WEEK:

WHO WILL WIN THE NEXT WORLD SERIES:

---

design a database for inventorying household items or recording food storage. Suggested time: two sessions.
4. Participants become familiar with graphing programs by ex-
   amining prepared graphs and constructing computer-
   generated graphs using data from their workplace or home life.
   Suggested time: two sessions.
5. The purposes and values of spreadsheets are recognized as
   learners order from a fast food menu (see Figure 4.2), prepare a
   budget (see Figure 4.3), and use spreadsheet capabilities to explore "what-if" decisions. Suggested time: two sessions.
6. Learners are introduced to programming by modifying programs (such as the BASIC program in Figure 4.4) and by creating
   geometric shapes (such as the Logo example in Figure 4.5). Suggested time: two sessions.
7. Several brands of computers can be brought in for learners to
   explore the similarities and differences of equipment and their
   operations and to become acquainted with other types of software such as text adventures, simulations, music, and art.
   (Ideas for this session are elaborated later in the chapter.) Suggested time: one session.
8. In addition to evaluating growth during the course, the final

FIGURE 4.2   A Spreadsheet with Fast Food Data

	Quantity	Unit Price	Total
Item			
Fastburger	2	1.49	2.98
Fast Fries	1	0.59	0.59
Instant Coffee	2	0.59	1.18
Hasty Pudding	1	0.79	0.79
Subtotal	----	----	5.54
Tax	----	----	0.22
TOTAL	----	----	5.76

FIGURE 4.3   Spreadsheet for a Home Budget

	Budget	Actual
Rent/Mortgage	450.00	450.00
Food	300.00	332.00
Utilities	100.00	93.48
Telephone	20.00	24.13
Car/Transportation	150.00	296.29
Entertainment	50.00	68.46
Savings	130.00	
TOTALS	1200.00	1264.36

FIGURE 4.4   An Example of a BASIC Program that Learners Can RUN, LIST, and Alter

```
100 PRINT"  *          *          *    *      ****"
110 PRINT"  *        *   *        *    *      *"
120 PRINT"  *        *    *       *    *      *"
130 PRINT"  *        *    *       *    *      *"
140 PRINT"  *        *    *       *    *      *****"
150 PRINT"  *        *    *        *    *     *"
160 PRINT"  *        *    *         *  *      *"
170 PRINT"  *          *   *         **       *"
180 PRINT"  *****      *             *        *****"
190 END
```

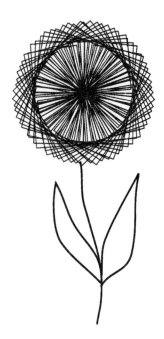

FIGURE 4.5   An Example of a Logo Design

session may include discussions about purchasing hardware and software and taking advantage of opportunities for continued learning to keep up with technology.

LESSON FORMAT

Because objectives and activities vary from session to session in a computer awareness course, the same format will not fit every lesson. However, some general guidelines can be given for beginning the session, introducing the topic for the day, providing hands-on practice, and concluding the session. Each of these parts of the lesson will be described and examples given in illustrative lesson plans.

Beginning the Session

Each class session starts with a planned activity that can be done independently with little or no instruction. Learners arrive for class at different times, so it is wise to plan ways to involve the early arrivals in meaningful practice. The activity should be short and must be one that will not penalize latecomers who do not have time for it. It could be a follow-up to the preceding lesson, providing both review and additional practice related to a particular concept or function. Alternatively, the activity might be one that will serve as an introduction to the lesson for the day. Some learners who arrive early will know what they want to practice; if so, they should feel free to do so rather than be obligated to do the planned activity.

The independent activity continues until all or most of the class members have arrived. In some cases, the teacher might decide to let the participants continue to practice for a while, depending on the needs and the involvement of the learners. At other times, the lesson for the day might begin shortly after all learners have arrived. If the opening activity is one that will provide a lead-in to the day's lesson, of course it will be necessary to make sure that the last person to come to class has a chance to get acquainted with it.

Introducing the Topic

The first "formal" part of the lesson is an off-computer activity, a guided hands-on activity, or a demonstration, depending on the experiences of the learners in relation to the topic. No matter what form the introductory activity takes, it is designed to convey to people the general content and purpose of the lesson. They should be guided to see how their background knowledge, from either life experiences or prior computer lessons, relates to the concept under study.

If the concept to be introduced is one that will be quickly and clearly grasped, an off-computer activity is used to make connections with the learners' prior experiences. For example, the first session on databases might be introduced through the use of a set of file cards containing recipes or inventories of sporting equipment or record collections. When a graphing program is used, people might first enter information on several large laminated charts, which will provide data for the computerized graphs to be developed. For example, they can record distances driven to work each day, favorite ice cream flavors, preferred pizza toppings, shoe sizes, or teams favored to win the World Series or Super Bowl.

For concepts in which the learners have limited background, a guided hands-on activity is desirable. For example, they will probably have limited knowledge about disk management operations, so this topic might be one in which they are guided step by step through the process. If the purpose is to make a backup copy of a word processing file disk, the teacher can guide class members in loading the disk operating system and systematically following screen commands for copying a disk. The teacher will need to explain each step briefly so the learners understand the meaning of the screen directions.

In some situations, a demonstration accompanied by class discussion is an effective way to begin a session. A demonstration might be an appropriate way to introduce a lesson on the creation of a simple database. Typically, a session on the creation of a database follows one in which prepared databases have been used. Learners can be encouraged to recall the types of items included on the prepared databases and use the ideas as a springboard to thinking about other types of information that might be included on a database, such as one for a household inventory. Using one of the suggestions from the class, the teacher can demonstrate the creation of a new database form on the computer.

Providing Practice

Most of the lesson time should be spent in hands-on practice. One learns to read by reading, to write by writing, and to use a computer by using a computer.

The success of the lesson often depends on the particular practice activities provided. For some topics and for some people, the suggestion to "go ahead now and see what you can do" is all that is needed. For others, however, this is not sufficiently challenging. Furthermore, replicating a demonstration or exploring randomly might not lead to an awareness of the merits and possibilities of the particular software program or activity. Therefore, practice activities must be carefully designed and organized so they are interesting and purposeful. Activities should be planned that provide some challenge to the learner's thinking, but not so much challenge as to be frustrating.

In addition, the activities must be adaptable to the range of individual differences in backgrounds and interests of class members. One way to do so is to design activities that are fairly easy at the beginning but that can be pursued to higher levels as the computer user becomes comfortable with the lesson and the equipment. Learners who take longer or who simply want to become more proficient can pace themselves, without feeling any pressure to undertake additional exercises. Optional extension activities can be planned and suggested on an individual basis to learners who have grasped the concept and are ready to investigate more possibilities with it.

Another way to provide for differences is to encourage learners to interact with one another. Occasionally activities are planned in which two people are expected to work together. Whether the interaction is planned or incidental, learners should be encouraged to seek and offer suggestions or support to those working at the next computer. Teachers often remark about how they really understood a particular topic once they began to teach it; this learning-by-teaching strategy can be used in the computer classroom, too. Of course, the teacher is always there to provide help, answer questions, or, better yet, *ask questions that will help the learner think through the solution to a particular situation.*

In some lessons, the practice phase will be divided into parts, with brief demonstrations or explanations alternating with short practice sessions. While this format is a little harder to manage, primarily because of the differences in learners' response times, it is sometimes essential. If the lesson is not broken up into meaningful segments, the learners can feel so overwhelmed by getting too much information that they feel out of control when they turn back to the keyboard.

Concluding the Session

Whenever possible, lessons should be concluded with a wrap-up. This provides an opportunity to review the major concepts for the day, get feedback from the learners about the value of the activity, share comments about the benefits of a particular application program, and answer questions.

There will be times, however, when a formal wrap-up is omitted. Sometimes hands-on activities will be continued until individuals feel satisfied that the objective has been accomplished or until time runs out. Of course, all lessons are planned so that each learner can reach the basic objective. If the teacher senses that the objective has not been met for some class members, a brief private discussion is held with individuals to ascertain their comfort level. A mental note is made as to what might be the reason, so that lessons can be revised, encouragement and support can be offered, and a special eye can be kept on the learner during the next class. Occasionally the learner will accomplish the objective and simply wants to continue to practice or explore. Thus, running out of time does not necessarily indicate that the learner has a problem; sometimes the only "problem" is a desire to keep working because the activity is so interesting or challenging.

Whether or not there is a formal wrap-up to the session, learners can be given a handout that summarizes the key concepts for the lesson. Not only does a handout help learners remember the concepts, it gives them a mini-reference manual. Some people keep this handout in a binder, which they bring to class each session. They might take it home and use it as a stimulus for talking with family and friends about their new insights. Samples of handouts are included with the three illustrative lesson plans that follow.

ILLUSTRATIVE LESSON PLANS

Three sample lessons will be described in the pages that follow:

1. a session on getting started
2. an introductory session on word processing
3. a session on using several brands of computers

These sessions will illustrate adaptations of the general lesson format just described.

The first lesson offers some ideas about setting the tone and creating a supportive environment at the outset of the course. In the second, suggestions are made for introducing word processing through a meaningful activity; this lesson serves as a model for the use of a reality-based activity as the means for introducing *any* application program. The third lesson is unique in proposing that learners be exposed to additional types of hardware and software in order to help them realize that their skills and knowledge are transferable to other equipment and situations.

Getting Started

Learners arrive with a wide range of information, knowledge, skills, and concerns about using computers. During the first class (as in all sessions) the teacher should be alert to indications of the learners' feelings of confidence and levels of anxiety. Many insights will be gained by watching as they pursue the goals for this session: becoming familiar with the keyboard and running menu-driven programs.

Lesson Objectives. During the getting started session, learners will

- associate terms with parts of the computer
- run menu-driven programs
- boot a disk
- use selected function keys
- create and print a sign

Preparation. The equipment and supplies must be ready before the learners arrive. Preparation will involve sharpening pencils and making sure sufficient copies of any print materials, such as a questionnaire and a handout for the session, are readily available.

Each computer is booted with one game disk or other easy-to-use, menu-driven program before the learners enter the classroom. Most computers come with an introductory tutorial disk; often such a disk includes too much information at too fast a pace, but it might be provided as an independent activity for a few minutes at the beginning of the class. In addition, one disk-operating disk (if needed), one sign-making program disk, and a related reference card to help with commands are placed next to each computer.

Beginning the Session. Each person is greeted enthusiastically upon entering the classroom. If an assessment of initial knowledge and attitudes toward technology is to be used, the questionnaire is handed out as the learners enter. (See Appendix A for an example of a questionnaire that can be used for initial assessment and as an evaluation tool at the end of the course.) To reduce some of the anxiety related to "first-day jitters" and a paper-and-pencil test, the learner can be told:

1. the purpose of the questionnaire is to help you compare what you know now with what you will know at the end of this course,
2. the information is confidential, and
3. the teacher is available for help if there are questions about a word or how to mark the answers.

All of the above comments are necessary to try to alleviate some of the apprehensions of learners, many of whom come with concerns about educational settings and their own abilities to perform within these situations. Such comments are especially important when using an introductory questionnaire because it may look like a typical test and therefore may be very anxiety-producing. The learners need to know that there are no right or wrong answers and that the questionnaire will not be graded.

Also, the teacher should be prepared to respond to indications of differences in reading and writing competencies. Some learners may need help with recognizing some of the words. The teacher reads aloud discreetly any words requested by an individual. Even after hearing the word, the learner may not know its meaning, but is encouraged to respond to the item anyway, as he or she currently understands it. Other people may ask for clarification of the way a word is used in a computing context. Since one of the purposes of an assessment is to have learners realize how much they have learned during the course, the terminology should not be explained at this point; however, it is important that all learners know that they are not expected to understand the meanings of the words in a computing context yet.

As individuals complete the questionnaires, they can begin to work with an introductory tutorial disk while waiting for other class members to finish the items. To help them get started with the tutorial, the teacher can guide them to compare a typewriter keyboard with the computer keyboard. Their attention can also be called to the directions on the screen, and a brief explanation can be given on running the program and using special keys (such as ⟨RETURN⟩ or ⟨ESCAPE⟩).

Everyone should have an opportunity to use the tutorial program for several minutes before the teacher brings the group together for an overview of the course. Before the overview, however, the teacher can guide the group in taking out the disks and turning off the computers. By handling the disk and switches, learners have an initial experience with stopping and starting procedures, and the computers will be prepared for a hands-on experience with loading another program later in the lesson. (As an aside, it should be noted that in many computer labs, the switches are left on during the day, and the users do "warm boots" when changing programs. While the procedure is recommended and will also be taught, the learners need to realize where the switches are and how to operate them.)

Overviewing the Course. In order to establish a level of comfort and group cohesiveness, the teacher asks the learners what they think and, more important, feel about using computers. Through this discussion, people realize that others share the same feelings and apprehensions. Furthermore, the topic is one to which everyone can respond, which encourages them to speak within the group. The teacher's nonjudgmental acceptance of all responses helps create a positive learning environment. Introductions are also made at this time, helping learners get acquainted and giving the teacher an opportunity to practice the names. Perhaps each individual can share a personal piece of information and tell his or her purpose for taking the course.

Following this brief get-acquainted activity, the teacher explains that the main purpose of the course is to help people feel comfortable using technology to do what they want it to do for them. An alert and sensitive teacher can relate this overall goal to the individual purposes identified by the learners.

In most lessons a handout is provided at the end of the session to serve as a summary. However, for this lesson a handout might be distributed at this time to be used as a reference during the lesson. In the sample handout (Figure 4.6), the learners' attention would first be brought to the bottom of the page, where the attendance information is explained. The lesson might continue with a brief look at the other items on the handout. In relation to items 1 and 2, the term "boot" is defined and the learners can be assured that they

FIGURE 4.6 Handout for "Getting Started" Lesson

Computer Awareness Handout
Session 1

On the first day of class, I . . .

1. turned the computer on and off.

2. booted a disk.

   Booting means starting or restarting the Disk Operating System (DOS). This means putting a disk in Drive A (the drive on the left or on top), then turning on the computer switch.

3. identified the similarities and differences between a typewriter keyboard and a computer keyboard.

4. named parts of a computer system:

   keyboard   disk drive
   monitor   printer
   system unit

5. used menu-driven software programs to become familiar with the keyboard and create a sign.

* * * * * * * * * * *

Notes about Class Attendance

If you attend 14 or more sessions, you will earn a certificate to be received at the next Awards Ceremony. If you attend 15 or 16 sessions, there will be a gold seal on your certificate.

You can make up classes at another class time when the same lesson is being done. You can also come in any time on Fridays to do a missed lesson. The lab is open from 8:30 a.m. to 4:30 p.m. on Fridays, unless otherwise posted.

You are welcome to use the computers on Fridays for practice or for personal business.

---

will be booting the computers. As indicated by item 3, the differences between the typewriter keyboard and computer keyboard are reviewed. The hardware components, listed in item 4, are identified and their functions mentioned. In addition, the proper handling of a disk is demonstrated.

Continuing the Lesson. Enough talk. It is time to return to the computers. A group guided activity is used to involve learners in booting and using a menu-driven program. A sign- or poster-making program is a good choice that leads to a meaningful activity for using the keyboard and responding to menus. The teacher provides step-by-step directions for each person to load the program and begin to use the menu to create a sign. Examples of posters or signs are shown so that learners are aware of some of the decisions that need to be made in developing a finished product. To encourage independence even at this early stage, the teacher steps back and lets the learners proceed on their own, assuring them that help is available if needed. Meanwhile, the teacher circulates and encourages learners who are in need of assistance to think through what they are attempting to do (see teaching suggestions discussed in the section "Reading Issues" on pages 82–84).

Concluding the Session. Invariably people will finish designing their signs at different rates, so it is probably best to assist them individually when they are ready to use the printer. When the first ones finish their printing, they might help others with the process. The finished sign provides family and friends with proof that the learner actually used a computer, and, more important, it gives the creator a feeling of satisfaction and accomplishment.

A nice informal ending to this first lesson might be to encourage learners to express their feelings about using computers and their reactions to the day's activities.

Introducing Word Processing

Because typing is a familiar concept to almost everyone, word processing is perhaps the best of the application programs with which to start. It can be introduced after a session or two in which learners have had an opportunity to get familiar with the keyboard and to use some menu-driven programs. Introducing word processing early in the series of lessons also provides an opportunity for learners to create and print texts that are purposeful, such as letters to friends or relatives.

Lesson Objectives.   During the first session devoted to word processing, learners will

- explain what word processing is
- enter and save a personal letter
- clear the memory (RAM)
- retrieve a file from the disk
- insert words into text

Preparation.   In preparation for the lesson, the teacher places beside each computer one copy of the required disks: DOS (if needed), the word processing program, and a formatted file disk. One or more large wall charts with the directions for booting the word processing program should be prominently displayed. An example of such a chart is shown in Figure 4.7. Printouts of a paragraph are prepared so that learners have text to enter on the word processor at the beginning of the session. If a handout is to be distributed at the end of the lesson, copies should be ready.

Beginning the Session.   So learners can focus first on word processing functions rather than booting procedures, the word processor might be loaded on each machine to the point where a blank screen is available for entering text. As learners arrive, they can read the paragraph below and follow the directions in it.

> Today you will learn what a word processor does. Go ahead and type this paragraph on the computer. Just type the words and don't worry about mistakes. Do not use the return key when you get to the right side of the screen. WATCH THE CURSOR MOVE THE WORD TO THE NEXT LINE FOR YOU.

Some people need assurance that typing errors are expected and can be corrected easily later. As the sample paragraph indicates, they should type without using the RETURN key, with the intention that they will become aware of the wrap-around feature. Observant teachers will note that learners, especially those who have had some typing experience, often try ingenious techniques to get the cursor to the next line without using the RETURN key. While the temptation is to explain the wrap-around feature to such individuals during this early exploration, it might be better to let them

FIGURE 4.7   Chart, or Boot Board, with Instructions for Loading
a Word Processing Program

Boot Board

1. Boot DOS.

   Put DOS in drive A.

   If the machine is off --
       turn on machine.

   If the machine is on --
       press CTRL-ALT-DEL.

2. Enter date <RETURN>.
   Enter time <RETURN>.

3. Take DOS out of drive A.

4. Put word processing program in drive A.
   Type "key word" to load word processing program.
   Press <RETURN>.

5. Put file disk in drive B.

---

make some discoveries on their own. Anyone who is really frustrated can be offered the suggestion just to keep typing, without using any keys to move to the next line, and watch what happens on the monitor.

Speedy typists who complete the paragraph before the other class members have done so are encouraged to continue typing anything of their own choosing. They might try to figure out how to correct any typing errors by using some of the editing keys on the computer (BACKSPACE, arrows, DELETE).

Introducing the Concept.   When all learners have finished entering the paragraph, the teacher has them gather around one monitor for a discussion about the concept of word processing and the features of the program being used. An explanation of word processing can be elicited from the group, supplemented by teacher comments. The wrap-around feature and cursor movement can be explained and demonstrated briefly.

The various commands shown on the screen can be mentioned to create an initial awareness of the options available. Because word processors vary, it is impossible to tell exactly what commands deserve attention. The commands on some screens will be relatively clear and easy to interpret. Others may appear to be simple on the surface, but the choice of one command may bring up a sub-directory with a lot of information that is not essential at this early stage. A knowledgeable teacher will anticipate this and focus only on the few essential commands for entering and editing text. Learners should be assured that other features will be introduced as needs arise.

On some word processors, the screen will show the extent to which the random access memory (RAM) is full. Learners are usually interested in knowing that this means their text is taking up a certain amount of space in the computer's memory, but this is hardly the time to go into a lengthy discussion of the internal workings of the machine or even a clarification of RAM and ROM (read only memory). In most cases, explanations of such concepts are better left until later in the course, when people have had many opportunities to save materials on disks and to realize where their texts really are residing both before and after saving them. The explanation about the features of the word processor should be short and functional. The learners should get back on the machine as soon as possible.

A meaningful activity that will give learners practice using a word processor is writing a letter to a friend or relative—a real letter that, upon completion, will be mailed or delivered in person. The teacher needs to demonstrate how to clear the practice paragraph so that the screen is clear for the letter to be written. The teacher can also demonstrate the typing of a greeting for a letter, such as "Dear Mom," and show that the RETURN key is used after the salutation in order to go down two lines to start the letter.

Continuing the Lesson. Each learner can now return to a machine, clear the screen, and begin working on a letter. The participants should understand that the emphasis is on the message and that the material will be saved for the next session so that revising and editing can be done then.

Individuals will finish at different times, so it is probably best to show the procedure for saving on the disk to each person as he or she completes the letter. The learner is guided to insert the formatted file disk into a disk drive and follow the directions for saving a file. Once again, it is important to encourage the learner to make predictions and think about the meaning of the terms and the menus, rather than simply follow the teacher's directions. Attention should be called to the red light on the disk drive so the learner realizes that text is being transferred to the disk.

The first people to finish might help others save their letters. However, the teacher should watch this step carefully and be ready to step in if there seems to be confusion. While it is not easy to erase the letter from memory, it is possible—and it is disheartening to lose a file at any time, especially during this first attempt. Another option for those who finish early is to clear the memory and compose another letter.

Concluding the Session. After everyone has finished saving, the group can be reassembled. Now is a good time to talk briefly about computer memory, both within the machine and on the disk. The learners are reminded that their letters have been filed away on the disk so they will be able to get them back for further use during the next session.

Many people have difficulty understanding the difference between having their text in the computer memory and having it saved on the disk. The following procedure is one way to help learners begin to understand this concept. Using a sample letter (of a learner who doesn't mind having his or her work viewed), the teacher moves the cursor somewhere in the middle of the text and enters some random letters, perhaps a series such as "zzzzzzzzzz." After the text in memory has been altered, the teacher demonstrates how to recall the original file from the disk. The learners will see that the original version has now reappeared intact, without the distortions that were inserted in the demonstration. Many learners will still be confused about the location of the text and how the unaltered version has reappeared, but they are usually relieved to find that the original text has been saved and can be recalled from the disk.

To demonstrate the ease of making revisions, the teacher can insert words or sentences within the text. Using the same letter of that confident writer, the teacher can have the learners suggest another sentence to incorporate within the first paragraph, then show how to move the cursor and type in the text. Observing the screen, the learners will note that the rest of the text simply moves to accommodate the added information. On some computers and software programs, the teacher will have to alert learners to the use of the INSERT key or other command with which to change from inputting new text to replacing, or typing over, letters and words.

If time permits, learners can return to their own letters and experiment with inserting text. They might also look at the HELP menu and experiment with their letters, using some of the additional features that they discover. Once again, they are assured that their original letters have been safely filed away on the disk for revision and editing in the next lesson.

At the close of the session, learners are guided to return to the main menu (or whatever the particular program requires) in order to quit the program and remove the disks. With some application programs, notably databases, data can be destroyed if the proper steps are not followed to close files before leaving the program, so it is wise to have learners get in the habit of using the appropriate "quitting" routine.

As the learners prepare to leave, they are sent off with a forward look to the next session, when they will edit, have the computer check their spelling, and print their letters. A handout, such as the one in Figure 4.8, can be distributed as a reminder of the features of this lesson.

Using Other Computers

During this session, one of the last in the course, learners can get acquainted with computers other than those they have been using. The purposes of the session are to help learners realize they have the skills to use whatever computer they wish and introduce them to other types of software having unique features that may not have been demonstrated during other class sessions. This lesson could

FIGURE 4.8 Handout for the First Session on Word Processing

Computer Awareness Handout
Word Processing: Creating and Saving Text

Today I . . .

1. used a word processor to write a draft of a letter.

   The word processor is an application program that turns the computer into a fancy typewriter. With a word processor, I type in information, then make all of the corrections on the screen before printing out the final copy.

2. learned where information is within the computer.

   a. When I first type a paragraph, the information is stored within the temporary memory (RAM).

   b. Then I save the paragraph on a file disk. My paragraph is now in two places:

      (1) in the temporary memory and
      (2) on the disk.

   c. Now I can clear the temporary memory (RAM) and get a "clean page" to create another document. My first paragraph is still on the disk.

   d. If I want to see my first paragraph again, I can get a copy of it from the disk.

---

also become a preparation for a session that will focus on decision making about purchasing a computer.

The lesson is best done in pairs or small groups so that the adults may share in the interaction naturally generated by using different types of software and keyboards. Pairing or small groups may also be necessary due to the limited number of other computers available.

Lesson Objectives. During this session, the learners will

- use a variety of educational software
- experiment with computers of brands other than those regularly used in the class
- compare the disk operating systems and loading procedures among the different computers

Preparation. In preparation for the lesson, the teacher needs to borrow at least three different types of computers that have not been used in class. The computers are brought into the classroom and set up prior to the beginning of class. These additional computers can be borrowed from a variety of sources: computer stores, educational institutions, or the teacher's or learners' homes.

One or two software programs should be borrowed to run on each computer. This lesson provides an opportunity to bring in types other than the application programs used in the class, such as text adventures, interactive educational programs, simulations, and software incorporating music, speech, or drawing. The software may be selected to include ideas that the learners have indicated as ways they would like to use the computer, such as for helping their youngsters or organizing information about hobbies. Booting directions for each program are written on a card and placed with each piece of software. A handout such as Figure 4.9 might be prepared for this session.

Beginning the Session. Learners can be told that they will work with different computers during the class period. They can select one of the programs placed beside a selected computer and follow the booting instructions provided. As others arrive, they are encouraged to join those already at one of the computers.

Continuing the Session. After 10 to 15 minutes at a station, the learners are encouraged to move to another brand of computer.

FIGURE 4.9 Handout for a Session on Using Other Computers

Computer Awareness Handout
Other Computers

Today I . . .

1. tried several adventure programs on the

   _____ computer.

2. tried a flight simulator and a music program on the

   _____ computer.

3. watched a demonstration of the mouse and a

   drawing program on the _____

   computer.

4. learned the similarities and differences in loading

   and running software programs on various computers.

5. talked about the similarities and differences among

   the brands of computers on the market.

They may wish to continue using the software already loaded there or load a different program. If they choose one already loaded, then one of the original users can explain what is happening before moving to another computer. By the end of an hour all participants should have had an opportunity to work with each machine. During this hour, the teacher can rotate from one group to another, asking questions when needed to guide the use of the programs and answering questions posed by learners.

After an hour, the learners might convene as one large group to discuss the similarities and differences noticed while moving from computer to computer and program to program. The learners' feelings of comfort and ability to use the different computers and programs can be discussed. The teacher might help the learners recall that their questions while they were using the computers were not, "How do we use this computer?" but were related to the program content; for example, "How do we get the truck started?" or "How do we find out the best country to go to next?" Such a discussion is a means of helping learners realize that each time they encounter a new piece of software, they must go through a process of getting to know the specific commands for that program.

The variations in booting procedures can also be discussed at this time. The teacher can have the learners describe the booting procedure for the computer they normally use during the class and compare this information with the way each of the other computers boots; not all learners will have booted a different computer or thought about the relationship of the booting process to that of the computer they have been using regularly. To emphasize the different booting procedures, the teacher could demonstrate them once more by introducing an additional piece of software for each computer, perhaps one with a special feature such as a speech synthesizer.

Often the experience with other computers will lead to questions about which is best or which one a person should buy. This would allow the teacher to point out the similarities and differences among the various brands. These potential purchasers should be alerted to the first question that needs to be answered when considering a purchase: What do I want a computer to do for me? Each individual must realize that a wise decision about buying a computer can be made only after one has determined the purpose(s) it will serve.

Concluding the Session. After all the demonstrations are concluded, the learners are encouraged to talk about their feelings about using the different computers. Also, this might be a good time to review the many types of software programs that are available.

SPECIAL CONSIDERATIONS

When planning a computer course, several factors must be taken into account: teacher-learner-computer ratios, open lab times, software selection, and learner-produced materials. Suggestions for each of these are offered in the following paragraphs.

Teacher-Learner-Computer Ratios

In order for the teacher to be alert to the needs of learners and to facilitate their personal involvement in each lesson, class size must be considered. Obviously, the lower the ratio, the more personal attention can be given. However, the class size should be large enough to take advantage of the experiences of a number of adults with diverse backgrounds. Even though learners will work in pairs at some times, most adults prefer to have their own computer so that they can have maximum hands-on experience. Given these considerations, a class size of 10 learners with 10 computers is suggested. With this number, a lead teacher and an assistant are desirable so as to be able to observe comfort levels and provide immediate assistance as needs arise. This level of staffing may not be possible but would be ideal. Volunteers from the community and from former classes or cooperative education students from local colleges might be recruited as assistants; they will, of course, need to become familiar with the framework and teaching approaches of the program.

Open Lab Times

Because of numerous responsibilities, adults are not always able to attend every class session. For this reason, open lab time should be provided. If computer classes for adults are held on-site or in an adult education facility, one day a week might be set aside when no classes are scheduled so that learners can make up missed sessions. This time might also be used for learners to get additional practice or to explore application programs on their own.

Software Selection

In a computer awareness course the intent is that adults become familiar with the features of the major types of application programs rather than attempt to learn all the intricacies of specific software packages. Therefore it is wise to choose programs that are easy to use, rather than introduce the latest state-of-the-art materials with more capabilities than most people need in order to become comfortable with computers. Menu-driven programs, in which the commands are on the screen, are easier than command-driven programs, in which special codes must be inserted for such features as centering, underlining, and setting margins. Furthermore, it is helpful to purchase the major application programs from the same company, if possible, so that the menus and commands are similar from one package to the next.

Learner-produced Materials

As often as possible, learners should create materials during the lessons that can be printed and taken with them. While the emphasis is on the process of learning, nonetheless it is very satisfying to have a product for oneself and to show others. Products that serve a real function prove very rewarding. In classes where such products have been created, adults have had many heartwarming experiences. For example, love letters have been written to surprise spouses, and notes have been sent to renew contacts with far-away friends. Word processed articles compiled in a newspaper have been proudly shown to co-workers and family. As a matter of fact, learners have been known to request a clean copy of the newspaper to take home, because the first copy was smudged from its handling by interested fellow workers.

SUMMARY: PEOPLE USING COMPUTERS CONFIDENTLY

A course planned around the major application programs—word processing, databases, spreadsheets, and graphing—provides a meaningful context in which learners realize the functions computers serve, become familiar with terminology, and become confident in using the equipment. Everyone can become comfortable with computers, given sensitive teachers and well-designed lessons. Teachers who are responsive to people's feelings about technology and knowledgeable about ways to meet differences in reading abilities will build upon learners' efforts, guide and support their discoveries, promote their active involvement in hands-on activities, and encourage them to enhance their learning by helping one another. Activities developed around real situations will build upon the wealth of background experiences adults bring to the computer class. Opportunities for discussions and writing will enable learners to apply their background knowledge to computer lessons.

The theme of this chapter, "getting comfortable with computers," is broader than "learning about computers." The underlying assumptions are that the outcome is not simply knowing, but doing; that learning is not mechanical, but meaningful; and that the center of attention is not machines, but people.

« 5 »

Integrating Computers
in Adult Literacy Programs

Computers can be used effectively as instructional tools in many areas of adult education. They can contribute in several ways:

1. motivate learners
2. make writing, revising, and editing easier
3. engage learners in gathering and organizing data and using the information to solve problems in math, science, and social studies
4. acquaint adults with the technology that has become so prominent in society and the workplace

This chapter focuses on the use of computers as instructional tools within the curriculum, in contrast to the material in Chapter 4, which describes a course designed specifically to help people become familiar with the technology itself.

Application programs such as word processors and databases have more potential than many commercial reading, writing, and GED software packages for enhancing adult literacy instruction. Word processing can be used to reinforce the connections between reading and writing. As added values, learners will practice the reading strategies necessary for using technology, become familiar with software menus, and learn to manage files, disks, and printers. Databases are used in many businesses and industries as a means of organizing, recording, and managing a wealth of information. Activities with databases will provide opportunities for adults to apply reading and writing strategies to common situations they will encounter in everyday life, and thus enable them to approach databases with confidence in local business places or in the workplace. The first two sections of the chapter are devoted to suggestions for incorporating word processing and databases into an adult education program.

Two other types of application software offer possibilities for adult education programs—spreadsheets and graphing programs. Both are used widely in the business and industrial world, and their use in instruction should not be overlooked. In the third part of this chapter, some suggestions are offered for meaningful learning experiences with these tools that will provide adults with practice on math concepts as well as introduce them to other facets of the technological environment they might encounter in various occupations today.

The last section of the chapter deals with commercial packages designed specifically for instruction. The use of computers simply as teaching machines is not advocated; such use is not consistent with whole language principles nor does it take advantage of the unique capabilities of the technology. Unfortunately, much of the packaged software designed for instruction currently is of the drill and practice type, with a focus on skill development or learning of facts rather than on meaningful interactive communication. Users are expected to attend to *products* (correct answers) rather than to thinking and learning *processes.* Many software packages marketed under a reading or language arts label are based on a subskills theory of reading that assumes that adults need persistent, independent, monitored practice on a sequence of skills. Nonetheless, some comprehension and vocabulary software programs are available that can be used in ways that are consistent with the principles of whole language. Guidelines are presented for selecting such software, several programs are described that come close to meeting the selection criteria, and suggestions are made for using those programs in interactive ways in reading and writing classes. In addition, examples are given of types of prepared programs that can contribute to the thinking and problem-solving processes required in science, social studies, and mathematics.

WORD PROCESSING AND RELATED SOFTWARE

Word processing, which is available for every computer on the market today, will help learners take advantage of the natural connections among reading, writing, and thinking. With word processors learners can type whatever they are thinking, with no concern for spelling, grammar, or format while the content is being formulated. They can easily insert, delete, and move text as revisions are made in the flow of thought. Writers can elaborate on ideas and experiment with language without trying to follow their thoughts through a muddle of cross-outs, erasures, carets, and arrows. Learners can use the word processor as a tool when brainstorming, clustering, taking notes, summarizing, and organizing materials. They can record personal anecdotes or reactions to readings (see Chapter 2); organize, synthesize, analyze, and apply concepts in social studies and science (see Chapter 3); and write original math problems or make notes about processes used in solving those problems (see Chapter 3). The writing process and the GED lessons described in Chapters 2 and 3 do not change significantly; they are simply enhanced through the use of this versatile tool.

Word Processing in Reading and Writing

Both the teacher and the learners can use the word processor as a tool. At first, teacher modelling of its use will be important. For example, during brainstorming about a topic, the teacher might gather a small group of learners around the computer and record their ideas. Multiple copies of the ideas can be quickly printed. The learners can then use those ideas as stimuli for their paper-and-pencil drafts. As learners become comfortable using the word processor, some may choose to enter their drafts directly into the computer rather than on paper. For others, the teacher might transfer the drafts to the computer after class in preparation for the next session, when revising and editing will take place (see Chapter 2).

Another use of the word processor is to record predictions about events in a story or to record learners' background knowledge and questions about the topic for the day. Here again, their thoughts could be entered on the computer by the teacher and saved on disk. After reading the story or informational text, the learners' initial thoughts and questions can be retrieved and printed so they can evaluate their predictions, add information, and make comparisons with information gleaned from other sources.

Perhaps the greatest value of the word processor occurs when writers revise and edit their texts. To illustrate this, let us look at the following example of a first draft an adult learner might write:

THIS IS MY STORY

In my life i had jobs werking with recreatin and in a hardware store and a warehouse supplier and i have been a forklift driver, assembler, selector. It has been wonderfil werking with the supply compny.

The content of this text is understandable. The writer has a message to convey about his work history, but it could be clarified and enriched with details. As a result of rereading the material and conferencing with the teacher and his peers, the writer can add details to produce the following version:

MY WERK EXPERENCES

In the yer 1963 i had a job werking with the recreatin dept where i werked for 7 yers and then i deside i wood take a job with a hardware store and i werk with them for atlest to year and then i deside to move and went to werk for a windo and door warehouse supplier where was i hired in 1972 and was laid of for 10 weeks and in the yerr of 1973 i where call back to werk and i have been a forklift driver, assembler, and a selector. It has been wonderfil werking with the supply compny.

When the writer is satisfied with the content, the editing can begin. Through oral rereading, the learner will quickly realize that "was i" is reversed and can decide where to divide the text into sentences. With the word processor capabilities, these changes are incredibly easy to make.

Spelling, Grammar, and Style Checkers

A spelling checker, a software program that identifies misspelled words, can be an invaluable aid during editing. With the spelling checker, each word in the text is compared with a list of words stored within the program. When an unknown word or suspected misspelled word is found, the checker will provide several options from which the writer must choose. Typically these options are

1. the word is spelled correctly and the search can be continued
2. not only is the word spelled correctly but it is one that is used regularly—such as a place name or a specialized term related to one's occupation—and it should be added to the list in the spelling checker
3. possible spellings for the word can be displayed, from which the correct one can be selected
4. none of the first three options applies and the user must enter the correct spelling.

Spelling checkers do not teach people how to spell nor do they make decisions about the proper word choice. They simply alert writers to possible problem spots. Used wisely and consistently, they can lead adults to develop an awareness of standard spellings and to become more confident about this aspect of writing. Some skeptics might argue that writers who cannot spell words when they write them will not be able to use a spelling checker effectively. Spelling a word from memory, however, is a different process than identifying a word from a list of choices. Furthermore, some of the misspelled words may simply be typing errors or oversights that occur because attention is on the message; the writer will quickly recognize such problems when they are highlighted.

As an example of the use of the spelling checker as an instructional aid, consider its use with the learner's passage above. One of the words that the spelling checker highlighted was "yer." When possible spellings were requested, six choices were displayed— year, yearn, yen, yes, yet, and your—and the writer easily identified the correct spelling from the list. The writer was certain that the word "werking" was spelled correctly; after discussing the choices presented by the checker with the teacher, he began to internalize the concept that in this case the "er" sound is spelled "or." The text has some errors that the spelling checker did not detect. For instance, "to," "wood," and "of" are all legitimate words, but they are not the appropriate ones for this context; the writer was guided to realize that he must not rely solely on the spelling checker for proofreading. Of course, words identified with the spelling checker and with the additional proofreading are all good candidates for vocabulary cards, as described in Chapter 2.

Software programs are available that will check for errors other than spelling. Grammar checkers will examine text and highlight potential problems such as homonyms, commonly confused words (affect/effect), overworked words (pretty, said), overuse of "to be" verbs, sexist terms, and missing members in pairs of quotation marks or parentheses. Style checkers might graph the length of sentences and paragraphs so that the reader can detect whether they are consistently long or short. Some programs will display sentences vertically or in a graphic form so that the writer can evaluate the variety in sentence patterns and the use of conjunctions and transition words. Other programs will display an outline of the written document, that is, the first sentence from each paragraph, for the writer to determine whether the flow of the text is coherent. As with spelling, writers must decide what to do with the information provided by grammar and style checkers.

A learner would not be expected to use all of the checking programs at a given time. Adults working on basic literacy development might be guided to use only the spelling and homonym checkers as one aid for vocabulary development and word recognition skills. Adult learners in a GED program, on the other hand, might use style checkers as an aid to organizing and summarizing science and social studies content in a logical and coherent manner.

With or without spelling and grammar checkers, teachers and learners working through the revising and editing processes over a period of time will discern a pattern of needs specific to the individual. Special lessons can be planned to address these areas of difficulty. When the learners' writings are done on a word processor and saved on disk, these special lessons can easily be created from their texts. For example, learners can expand their vocabularies and make their writings more interesting by using the search and replace feature of the word processor to substitute synonyms for overworked words. A lesson to help learners express ideas in alternative ways might be created by having them use word processing features to combine or otherwise restructure sentences in order to clarify the meaning and get variety in sentence types. They can move sentences or paragraphs to enhance the logical flow and coherence of the composition.

Publishing

Finished products evolving from word processing activities give evidence of progress and accomplishments. The individual might print out and compile a collection of writings in a notebook to savor over time and see how much growth has occurred. The articles might be shared with friends and classmates. Personal letters, business letters, and letters to the editor can be written and mailed. Selected writings can be printed in a newspaper or magazine format for distribution to others in the adult learning program as well as to family, friends, and co-workers (Young & Irwin, 1988). While many of these activities are possible without computers, they are easier and more professional looking with word processing. Furthermore, they might be enhanced with letterheads, newspaper mastheads, columns, and graphics made possible with printing programs and desktop publishing software.

DATABASES

A database is a computerized collection of information on a specific topic. A database file is developed around a category, such as personnel or inventory, and includes a separate record for each unit within the category, such as an individual employee or a specific stock item. Each record has a number of details (fields) related to that subtopic. A database on personnel, for example, would contain one record for each employee, and each record might have details such as name, address, phone, age, date of initial employment, job classification, department, salary, and number of dependents. An inventory database would contain one record for each item carried by the company, with details about number in stock, cost, selling price, supplier, and location in the warehouse.

Databases can be distinguished from other organized sources of information, such as telephone directories, recipe books, and library card catalogs, in that they can be searched rapidly and the information can be organized and reorganized for different purposes. The database can be used to locate quickly specific information such as a certain employee or stock item. It can be searched for all records containing particular details, such as employees making less than a given salary or items purchased from one vendor. Reports can be quickly generated, perhaps an alphabetical list of employees and addresses for mailing labels or an inventory list by department showing the number and value of items currently in stock.

Rationale for Using Databases

Databases sound like business tools. Why should they be used in an adult literacy program? One answer is that databases are commonly found in the workplace and in society; people today must know how to access them. Many computer terminals in businesses and factories are linked to databases. In some occupations—such as bank tellers, travel agents, and clerks in fast food stores—databases are integral parts of the daily routine. In other jobs employees are expected to use them for such tasks as maintaining accounts of hours worked or miles traveled, recording information about production, or locating stock items for repairing or replacing equipment. If people do not use databases in their jobs, they will use them outside the workplace—to access bank accounts from automatic tellers, check the stock and place orders at local discount stores, take advantage of speedy checkouts at motels, locate information in a library, and order goods or airplane tickets from a local or national communications network. By being exposed to database activities within the adult literacy program, learners will gain confidence in functioning in the many situations in which this technology is being used today.

If the fact that databases are used widely in society is not reason enough, their use is justified within the instructional program as a way to teach and practice a number of reading and study skills. When learners are guided through meaningful search activities with prepared databases, they will be engaged in following directions, determining key words, expanding vocabulary by thinking of synonyms, comparing data, making inferences about relationships among items of information, and raising questions about the significance of various factors related to a topic. When learners add information to databases, they will be involved in locating appropriate reference books, using indexes, scanning for specific details, classifying information, and verifying spellings.

Introducing Databases

Database application software programs are similar to word processors in that they are open-ended and thus easily adapted to the users' purposes. With word processors, users enter and edit their own texts; with databases, users develop files and enter information that can be searched and sorted according to their needs and interests. Databases, like word processors, come in all levels of sophistication—including some with far more features than are needed for instructional purposes. If database programs are already available at the site or are to be purchased, the teacher and learners should be expected to use only the appropriate features and should not be overwhelmed by all of the characteristics that an eager salesperson or a technical computer trainer might want to present. Regardless of the program, forms for instructional purposes can be created within a matter of minutes by merely typing in the names of the categories. Simple searches can be carried out without knowing all the possible search strategies.

An effective introduction to databases might be to have each learner enter personal information in a file, such as shown in Figure 5.1. Once the data from all class members are entered, the teacher can model search strategies, starting with such things as locating all those who live in the same zip code area or who have

FIGURE 5.1   A Database About Class Members

FIRST NAME: LAST NAME:

STREET ADDRESS:

CITY:

STATE: ZIP:

PHONE:

NUMBER OF CHILDREN:

MILES DRIVEN TO WORK:

FAVORITE FOOD:

PREFERRED TV NEWSCASTER:

FAVORITE VACATION SPOT:

---

similar tastes in foods. The learners might then be guided to conduct searches for the most popular newscaster or the person who has to travel the longest distance to work. The use of the database to print out address labels might also be demonstrated.

With the understandings gained from the use of a database about class members, learners will be able to enter information in files on other topics. Databases can be created on sports, automobiles, hobbies, local restaurants, community social service agencies, and job opportunities. A database on local places to visit, for example, might include information about the name of the place, its location, entrance fees, types of facilities, and other items of interest. After the learners have searched printed sources and entered appropriate information about local recreation facilities, they can be guided to search for places to go for hiking and fishing or for places to visit that can be reached within a particular time or budgetary constraint. Incidentally, the variety of ways in which people typically enter place names (Greenfield, Greenfield Village, Greenfield Museum, Henry Ford Museum, Fords museum, the muzeum in Dearborn) can lead to some good discussions about the need for standard spellings and consistency in entry format.

Reading and Writing Activities with Databases

Databases can be used to leave messages for others, thus providing another purpose for writing. Learners will eagerly search for messages from other class members or the instructor. A database form for this purpose can be very simple, including date, addressee, sender, and message. If the software program allows for more than one screen to a form, everything except the message can be put on the first screen. The message itself can then be written on the second screen, where it will be a bit more private. While paper and pencil are quicker for short notes, the advantage of a database is that the text will not be obscured by the handwriting, and the message can be edited easily without rewriting.

Databases might be used as tools for individual learners as well as for class activities. For example, they might be used as word banks. Vocabulary cards from learners' writings (see Chapter 2) might be kept in a computerized format. Everything that can be written on the 3 × 5 file card can be written on a database form. With the computerized word bank, the learner can search for the word as a spelling activity; to display the entry, the learner must spell the word correctly. In addition to the word, the form might include the original sentence from the learner's text as well as definitions, synonyms, and antonyms. If desired, a record of the number of times the word has been retrieved (thus spelled) successfully can be kept on the form. The word bank can be searched, sorted, and printed in whatever ways suit the learner's needs, such as an alphabetized list of all words being studied or file cards that can be carried in one's pocket or purse for study at home or during work breaks.

Still another use of the database is for keeping records of materials read, as illustrated in Figure 5.2. Learners can enter bibliographic information and comments about articles and books they have finished. Several reading skills are involved in completing this form, including summarizing, evaluating, and determining key words to represent main ideas. When the database is introduced, information about books or articles can be entered cooperatively through guided practice in small groups, based on materials that have been read in class. After learners are familiar with the form, they can enter information about their independent readings, search for sources on specific topics, or look for recommendations from people known to have interests similar to theirs.

FIGURE 5.2   A Database About Materials Read

TITLE:

AUTHOR:

SOURCE, IF ARTICLE:

PAGES, IF ARTICLE:

DATE OF PUBLICATION:

PUBLISHER, IF BOOK:

MAIN TOPIC:

RELATED TOPICS:

SUMMARY:

    :

    :

    :

EVALUATION:

REVIEWER:

Databases in GED Subject Areas

Databases are of special value in the content areas of adult literacy programs. For example, in social studies learners might develop a file of information about drugs or diseases. The development of the database would require the use of reading and writing skills to locate and summarize information to be entered. The completed database might serve as a reference for people who want to know about the symptoms and effects of various drugs or who want to know how to care for family or friends during an illness. The development and use of a database for this purpose would undoubtedly be accompanied by serious discussions about the need for entering accurate and adequate information. The database activity can be extended into a writing project. The learners might be guided to realize that compiling information in a database is a form of note-taking; the notes might become the basis for written reports to be assembled into a public service pamphlet and made available to interested people in the community.

If local or national issues are used as the focus for the reading and related writing phases of lessons, a database of politicians might be created—with fields for the person's name, title, political affiliation, address, committee assignments, and special interests. Reference materials and newspapers could be used to locate information to create the file. The database can then be used as a resource to determine appropriate officials to whom to address letters about issues discussed in class.

In addition to databases that the teacher (and perhaps the learners) develop, prepared databases are available. Many of them are based on topics in social studies and science. Some of these are in the public domain, for example, presidents, vice presidents, states, countries, U.S. economy, solar system, meteor showers, and geographic extremes (available for Appleworks from Teacher's Idea and Information Exchange, P. O. Box 6229, Lincoln, NE 68506). Others are available commercially, such as the activity packages from Scholastic Inc. (P. O. Box 7502, 2931 East McCarty Street, Jefferson City, MO 65102) on physical science, life science, weather and climate, U.S. history, U.S. government, the U.S. Constitution, and world geography and cultures.

In addition to using reference skills to add new information to files, learners can search and analyze material from prepared databases to discover relationships, formulate and test hypotheses, make interpretations, and draw conclusions. Obviously the value of using databases will be directly related to the types of questions asked and search strategies involved. For example, drawing conclusions about the relationships among population, products, and average salaries of people in various countries will be far more beneficial than merely sorting the countries according to whether they are primarily manufacturing or agricultural areas.

If accessible, the databases that are actually used in the community and the workplace might be investigated. Inventory data, sales records, gift registries, and customer name and address files are among the types of information that might be available for perusal. If such databases are not open to public view, valuable discussions about the issues of privacy can be stimulated, which might lead to some related reading and writing about ethical questions that people face because of the increasing use of computerized record keeping in our society.

Finally, if a modem is available learners might browse through some of the national databases. For example, they might search an on-line encyclopedia for the latest information on a science topic, use airline schedules to plan the most economical way to get to a vacation destination, or use a newspaper index to locate information about a controversial issue or political figure. Experiences of this type would have a direct effect on helping adults become aware of the need to adapt to changes in society, especially those brought about by technological developments.

SPREADSHEETS AND GRAPHING SOFTWARE

Spreadsheet programs are typically used for accounting and budgeting tasks in which numerical records must be made, calculated, and recalculated. Because of their nature, they will probably be used more in mathematics than in other areas of adult learning. Two simple spreadsheet examples are shown in Chapter 4 (Figures 4.2 and 4.3).

Spreadsheets can be used as an alternative to paper, pencil, and a calculator for setting up problems and computing results. The spreadsheet, like the calculator, allows learners to write the formulas needed for the operations. The computer will do the actual figuring so that the learner focuses on the process of finding the answer rather than simply on getting a right answer.

Math and Decision Making with Spreadsheets

To illustrate the use of a spreadsheet, recall the example in the math lesson in Chapter 3 in which the learners were to figure out the tip for a $5.15 restaurant bill. With a spreadsheet, the equation (formula) for the problem can be entered in the appropriate area (cell) and the computer will do the calculation. Each part of the equation should be labelled (see row 1 of Figure 5.3) so that the learners understand exactly what each equation represents (see row 3 of Figure 5.3). The equation B3 * .04 indicates that the food total of $4.95 found in column B, row 3 is multiplied (the asterisk denotes multiplication) by the state sales tax (.04 or 4%). To calculate the total bill in column D, the figures in cells B3 and C3 are

FIGURE 5.3 A Spreadsheet to Calculate Tips

=====A=======B=========C============D============E===				
1| DAY	FOOD	TAX	TOTAL BILL	TIP
2|				
3| Mon.	$ 4.95	B3 * .04	B3 + C3	C3 * .15
4|				
5|				
6|				
7|				
8|				
9|				

added together. Figure 5.4 shows the results of the calculations as they would appear on the screen.

The greatest advantage to using a spreadsheet within the curriculum, however, goes far beyond the calculation of simple problems such as tips. One of the benefits of a spreadsheet is that it allows the user to manipulate outcomes and answer "what-if" questions. For example, suppose a person wants to know how much it would cost to build a driveway. The information needed is: area to be covered, materials needed, the area that a given unit of material covers, and cost per unit for each of the materials. With

FIGURE 5.4 Calculations from the Formulas in the Spreadsheet in Figure 5.3

=====A=======B=========C============D============E===				
1| DAY	FOOD	TAX	TOTAL BILL	TIP
2|				
3| Mon.	$ 4.95	$ 0.20	$ 5.15	$ 0.77
4|				
5|				
6|				
7|				
8|				
9|				

this information, the problem can be set up to figure out the costs for each material for one square foot and then calculate the total amount of materials and costs based on the dimensions of the driveway. Setting up this problem, regardless of whether it is done on or off the computer, requires a lot of problem solving and developing of appropriate equations. With the spreadsheet, the user can speculate about the effect of making the driveway wider or thicker or of buying different grades of materials, by entering different amounts in the appropriate cells. Spreadsheet activities of this type can be used to explore relationships in many other situations, such as personal or national budgets, where it is often necessary to consider how to cover the impact of rising costs in one area by lowering expenditures in another area.

Activities with Graphing Programs

Graphs are pictures created to represent numerical information. With computerized graphing programs, learners can consolidate and enter data that will be displayed in visual formats as bar, line, or pie graphs. Graphs provide opportunities for identifying trends, making inferences, drawing conclusions, and hypothesizing about data. Interpreting and creating graphs involve analyzing and synthesizing information in new ways. While graphs are mathematical, the content is often related to data in science and social studies; graphing is an excellent way to prepare for GED tests in those subjects, since many of the sections require the examinees to interpret various types of adjunct aids, many of which are graphs.

As an example of introducing graphing using information from learners' experiences, consider the database activity described earlier in this chapter in which searches were made for the most popular newscaster or the person who traveled the longest distance to work. A graph could easily be developed listing the newscasters and showing the number of people who indicated a preference for each. Similarly, the number of people who drive 0–4, 5–9, 10–14, and more miles could be graphed.

Spreadsheet information can also be represented graphically. Suppose that a person regularly ate lunch at a restaurant and kept track of the amount spent each day in a spreadsheet such as shown in Figure 5.5. A pie graph such as Figure 5.6 can be created to show the percentage of the lunch budget that goes for taxes and tips in comparison with the cost of the food itself. A formula could be added to the spreadsheet to calculate the percentages, but the information is much clearer when graphed. This is a simple example

FIGURE 5.5 Spreadsheet of Weekly Eating Out Costs

=====A=========	B=========	C============	D============	E==
1| DAY	FOOD	TAX	TOTAL BILL	TIP
2|				
3| Mon.	$ 4.95	$ 0.20	$ 5.15	$ 0.77
4| Tues.	$ 5.79	$ 0.23	$ 6.02	$ 0.90
5| Wed.	$ 3.69	$ 0.15	$ 3.84	$ 0.58
6| Thurs.	$ 4.89	$ 0.20	$ 5.09	$ 0.76
7| Fri.	$ 5.39	$ 0.22	$ 5.61	$ 0.84
8|				
9| TOTALS	$24.71	$ 1.00	$25.71	$ 3.85

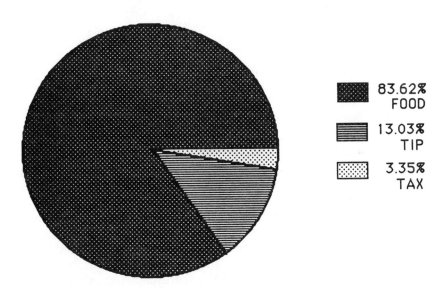

83.62% FOOD

13.03% TIP

3.35% TAX

FIGURE 5.6 A Graph of Weekly Eating Out Costs

to introduce the concepts of graphing and help learners become familiar with using a computer program to design the visual representation. From this beginning, the learners can go on to organize information, create graphs, and interpret data regarding budgets, sales in various departments, customer preferences for specific items or brands, number of nondefective items produced each day on factory lines, safety records in various parts of the plant, and many other categories of data that can be represented in a visual form.

SELECTING AND USING INSTRUCTIONAL SOFTWARE

In general, commercially packaged software should contain intact coherent texts, because it is only with meaningful content that real reading can occur. In a few cases drill and practice materials, carefully chosen and wisely used, might be interesting and motivational for some learners. Criteria for selecting software are given below, followed by examples of types of software currently available that seem to have the most potential for adult literacy programs. Sources for the programs mentioned are provided in the software section of the references.

Evaluation of Software

Figure 5.7 is a checklist for evaluating the content and strategies of reading software (adapted from the Michigan Reading Association, 1985). Software must have adult content and be based on a sound theoretical base that is consistent with current understandings of the reading process and the philosophy of adult learning underlying the instructional program. Interactive software programs are recommended. The term "interactive" means much more than entering answers to questions and receiving feedback as to their correctness; interactivity at such a low level does not foster higher-level thinking and the construction of meaning. Truly interactive programs will engage learners in inferring, analyzing, synthesizing, evaluating, and applying information. To promote these higher-level thinking strategies, the software must allow for re-reading and reflection. Although the features listed in Figure 5.7 apply to reading software, the same qualities should be sought in software for mathematics, science, and social studies. The quality of the documentation and the technical aspects of the software, while important, should be evaluated only if the materials satisfy the criteria for worthwhile content and valid learning processes.

Software to Promote Comprehension Strategies

At the time this book is written, relatively few software programs for adults meet the desired criteria. Several programs that have possibilities for meaningful interaction are described briefly to il-

FIGURE 5.7 Guidelines for Evaluating Reading Software

		Poor			Good
1.	Adult content, likely to be of interest	1	2	3	4
2.	Free of stereotypes (race, ethos, sex, politics, age, handicaps)	1	2	3	4
3.	Content can be modified by learner or teacher	1	2	3	4
4.	Accurate information	1	2	3	4
5.	Information organized and logically developed	1	2	3	4
6.	Formatting features aid comprehension (e.g., headings and spacings)	1	2	3	4
7.	Active reader participation required	1	2	3	4
8.	Skills practiced in real content with purpose	1	2	3	4
9.	Purpose(s) clear to reader	1	2	3	4
10.	Emphasis upon thinking rather than repetitive practice	1	2	3	4
11.	Time allowed for reflection and responses	1	2	3	4
12.	On-line aids available (e.g., dictionary)	1	2	3	4
13.	Accurate spelling, grammar, punctuation	1	2	3	4
14.	Provisions for transfer from computer to off-screen reading situations	1	2	3	4

Source: Adapted from Michigan Reading Association (1985). *Guidelines for evaluating reading software.* Grand Rapids, MI: Michigan Reading Association. Used with permission.

lustrate types of software that are being developed. Some of the software packages to be described have been designed for middle and secondary school students; they are included here to show the capabilities of the technology, even though such programs may not yet be available with adult content. Since the programming has already been done for adolescent learners, the insertion of adult texts would be relatively easy. In some programs, directions are provided to enable teachers or learners to enter their own texts, while in other cases the software company could be contacted and urged to create a version appropriate for adults. As educators demand higher-quality materials and consult with software producers in the development of them, the potential for using computers as instructional tools will increase.

The *Comprehension Connection* was designed specifically to engage learners in determining how well they understand a passage and, if they feel that comprehension is lacking, in selecting strategies they can use to gain meaning. The program contains short expository passages for which a number of on-line aids to comprehension can be accessed—an easier version, graphic aids, vocabulary, and main ideas for each paragraph. Although a series of multiple-choice questions must be answered before the reader can progress to another passage, the emphasis is not on supplying correct answers but rather on assessing one's level of understanding and using appropriate strategies to achieve comprehension. The *Comprehension Connection* is an example of the use of technology to offer readers immediate access to on-line assistance and supplementary information. As compact information-storage disks and interactive video become more readily available, the possibilities for immediate access to visual and auditory aids as well as to related text are enormous. In addition to access to prepared aids, programs are available in which users can develop their own aids, such as taking notes on the computer and referring to them as often as desired during the reading process.

Reading Realities is a series of software packages for secondary students who are potential dropouts. The materials are designed for readers who are functioning at a low level, but the content is directed toward real-world concerns of adolescents. Three themes are found within the collection of disks:

1. real-life dilemmas about issues faced by teens, for example, drugs, alcohol, cheating, pregnancy, and peer pressure,
2. career preparation in the form of biographies of people preparing to be secretaries, hairdressers, actors, attorneys, chefs, and computer operators,
3. actual court cases where the learner becomes the juror to decide cases about drunken driving, arson, sports tampering, and drug sales.

The learners are required to predict from the title and picture and again from the first screen of text. They can preview vocabulary or access definitions during reading. The user can choose to read word-by-word, by phrases, or a screen at a time. If a speech synthesizer is available, the words, phrases, or screen can be read with speech. With the word or phrase choices, the next word or phrase is underlined when the learner presses the arrow key. Following the reading, the learner can choose to answer multiple-choice questions, do cloze activities, answer five open-ended analytical questions, or respond to five creative questions in which the person thinks about the topic in relation to his or her own life. The analytical and creative questions are not scored, but a record can be made of the learner's responses to them. The questions would also lend themselves to dynamic group discussions.

The Puzzler is a software program based on the directed reading-thinking activity (DR–TA) in which readers make predictions and then read to evaluate and confirm or alter those predictions. In *The Puzzler,* predictions must be made before each new section of text can be accessed. After reading each portion of text, the user must evaluate the predictions before moving on. The reader must do the evaluating; the computer does not judge the appropriateness of any response. The texts for the original version of *The Puzzler* are for middle school students, but the software illustrates a strategy that is appropriate for all ages and is available with current technology. One might ask whether a computer is needed for the DR-TA strategy. The short answer to such a question is "no." The DR-TA is very easy for a teacher to implement and is equally easy for readers to use independently once they are aware of the value of predicting and confirming as a means of interacting with the author. However, using the computer to reinforce this reading strategy can provide variety in the instructional program and can be motivational as well.

The word "reinforce" is used deliberately in the preceding paragraph to indicate that this computer program, as with most software, will lose much of its value if it is handed to people as a way of instructing them by means of technology without human interaction. *The Puzzler* is not meant to be used independently to teach learners when and why to predict. The program can be used as an instructional tool for introducing prediction and evaluation strategies, and the teacher's guidance of related discussion during that introduction is important. One or two passages might be done as a group, with learners encouraged to make a variety of predictions and then read the text to verify and evaluate the ideas. After the learners are familiar with the strategy and its purpose, other passages in the computer program might be done without teacher intervention in order to provide practice in applying it. Even at the practice stage, however, independent use of the program might not be as beneficial as having two people working together and sharing their thoughts and reactions.

Software for Vocabulary and Word Recognition

Software programs that will automatically format cloze passages make it easy to provide practice on using context clues. Of course the teacher and learners must understand why cloze passages are being used and how they are related to the improvement of reading abilities. Among the values attributed to cloze activities are that learners will (1) become familiar with common letter combinations and practice spelling as they fill in letters in words, and (2) gain a greater facility with the use of syntactic (sentence structure) and semantic (meaning) clues as they determine suitable words within sentences. Such insights about word and sentence structure do not come automatically to many people; the teacher needs to interact with learners as they discuss why certain letter combinations or words are appropriate and as they verbalize how unknown words can be determined by the use of context.

M-ss-ng L-nks is a series of software programs that presents passages in cloze formats. Narrative texts are provided in the *M-ss-ng L-nks: Classics, Old & New* package, while expository texts are provided in *M-ss-ng L-nks: Microencyclopedia* and *M-ss-ng L-nks: Science Disk.* For more flexibility, the *M-ss-ng L-nks: English Editor* might be chosen since it allows the user to enter texts, which could be materials written by learners as well as passages from newspaper articles or other texts used in class. While some computerized cloze programs provide a limited number of formats, with *M-ss-ng L-nks* the formats can be varied in any way desired, such as deleting all vowels, all consonants, specific letters, every other letter, every other word, every *n*th word, or specific words. The initial or final letters of each word can be given, or the screen can be left entirely blank in order to re-create the whole passage with no clues. With all of these possibilities, the program can be used to meet a wide range of differences:

1. learners who need a lot of clues to help re-create their texts and who will benefit from practice on spelling the words they have used;
2. those who would profit from practice on the use of context

clues to determine appropriate function words (the, from, of, what, where, that, etc.);

3. those who could be challenged to expand their vocabularies and become aware of writing styles by thinking of synonyms and deciding which word was used by this particular author.

Other types of programs that would be appropriate for the practice phase of reading and writing lessons, as described in Chapter 2, might be ones designed specifically for spelling and vocabulary development. Computer programs are available (for example, *Wheel of Fortune*) in which users must fill in vowels and consonants to identify people, places, things, or phrases, as in the popular television game. Another software program that many adults like is *Hinky Pinky*, in which clues are given for rhyming words containing a given number of syllables. Many people enjoy figuring out that a hink pink (two words of one syllable each) for "group of workers who take care of animals" is "zoo crew," and a hinky pinky (two words of two syllables each) for "chocolate bar that has fallen onto the beach" is "sandy candy."

Programs that allow users to make their own materials might also find a place in an adult literacy program. Crossword puzzles to provide practice on vocabulary might be created with programs such as *Crossword Magic*. The teacher or the learner, or both working together, could easily create a puzzle based on words selected from a learner's story or from a topic for class discussion. The clues can be in the form of definitions, synonyms, or short cloze sentences. When learners are involved in creating the clues, they might find a real need to consult a dictionary or a thesaurus.

Many software programs are on the market for creating signs, posters, greeting cards, and letterheads. With these programs, learners might design birthday or holiday messages for family and friends, summarize favorite books in a poster format, or prepare personalized stationery for letters they will write. The finished products will give adults a sense of satisfaction, and in the process of creating the materials they will be engaged in following directions and becoming familiar with common commands for computer programs.

Problem-solving Programs

Problem-solving programs refer to software that involves learners in identifying problems and working through their solutions. They might be interactive text adventures, simulations, or programs with combinations of those features, which present learners with opportunities to explore and experiment with concepts. Examples of each of these will be given.

Computerized interactive text adventures offer interesting possibilities for meaningful reading practice. Interactive text adventures take the user on imaginary journeys to collect, deliver, or use articles to solve problems. Some programs require the user to enter words or phrases, while others provide a list of choices at each decision point. Some display the action with graphics, while others include descriptive sentences or paragraphs to explain the consequences of the user's actions. Because of their nature, such programs are highly motivational to some learners. In addition, they involve learners in predicting, making inferences, taking notes, and solving problems. Text adventures might be available for the uninterrupted sustained silent reading phase of the reading and writing lesson described in Chapter 2.

New interactive text adventures regularly appear on the market; any listing here would be quickly outdated. For teachers who are generally unfamiliar with adventure programs, one popular example might be noted—*Where in the World is Carmen Sandiego?* In this text adventure, clues must be gathered to track down thieves who have stolen precious artifacts from capital cities throughout the world. Although this adventure is fictional, it has implications for social studies in that it introduces facts about particular cities and countries. Furthermore, in using reference materials to interpret the clues, the learner practices skimming, scanning, using an index, and reading maps, charts, and tables. Other versions of this software take Carmen Sandiego and her cohorts on similar adventures in other parts of the world, including Europe and the United States.

Tom Snyder has produced some problem-solving courseware for mathematics that has interactive text adventure features. The programs entail solving a mystery or a problem, such as determining reasons for the uncanny rapid success of a museum in *The Secret of Vincent's Museum* and retrieving pirate treasure from the wreck of a sunken ship in *The Treasure of Fisher's Cove*. In order to get clues, the user must set up math problems, pinpoint relevant data for their solutions, and select appropriate arithmetic operations. The software is aimed at middle school ages, but the format has possibilities for adults. All that is needed is someone to design a similar program around an adult problem, such as declining production in a plant, disappearing funds from a business venture, or persistent unsupported rumors about an official in a local political office.

A program that might be used in a group setting to introduce the concept of interactive text adventures is *Birth of the Phoenix*. This tutorial adventure program comes with a 20-page manual that explains typical features of computerized adventures and gives suggestions as to how to communicate with the computer and how to respond in various problem-solving situations. The suggestions are important and useful guidelines, but they do not give specific answers—the user must make inferences, try synonyms, and draw conclusions. *Birth of the Phoenix* might be introduced before other adventure programs as a means of helping learners become familiar with appropriate problem-solving strategies as well as involving them in consulting documentation materials.

Simulation programs also involve comprehension strategies, for example, predicting, solving problems, taking notes, drawing conclusions, making generalizations, and comparing and contrasting information from other references. In addition, they can serve as the stimulus for writing activities. The main difference between interactive text adventures and simulations is that the former are based on fictional occurrences, while the latter re-create actions or situations that represent real events, perhaps with historical, economic, scientific, or political bases. The *Decisions, Decisions* series is a good illustration of such material; it includes programs on such topics as colonization, immigration, revolutionary wars, urbanization, foreign policy, television and media ethics, presidential campaigns, and the budget process. Many simulations take time and must be carried out over several days or sessions. For this reason, the programs that are selected should include provisions to save progress.

Some programs whose major purpose is to teach subject matter have been designed in ways that involve meaningful reading practice. For example, *Interviews with History* induces learners to conduct mock interviews to find out about historical figures. Interview questions are printed on reproducible sheets in the manual, and answers to the questions are sought by using the computer program as a source of information. To locate answers, the learner must choose questions or comments that appear on the screen beneath the graphic picture of the interviewee; for example, "How did you get started?" "How did your family feel about that?" "What did you do during the war?" "How did you become famous?" "Tell me more about that." "Shake your head and say 'I don't understand.'" Most screens also have a place where the interviewer can fill in a blank to ask a question, such as "Tell me about your _____." The learner must decide which questions to ask to get the desired information to record on the interview sheet. When satisfied that enough information has been gathered, the learner can choose to take the test. The test, when completed, is in the form of a summary paragraph about the character. If an incorrect answer is given, the program indicates the question to ask in order to locate the needed information and returns to the screen with the appropriate response.

Interviews with History could be used freely by the reader simply to explore avenues of interest about a character, perhaps during the silent reading phase of a lesson. In this case, the test is optional. Prior to using the program for independent reading, the teacher should model the procedure and conduct a group discussion about locating answers to specific questions. As a follow-up, learners can be guided to develop questions about other people (sports figures, television personalities, local union or government officials); consult books, newspapers, and magazines to locate answers; take notes; and write summaries or character sketches of the people. This might lead to writing autobiographical paragraphs, possibly to use for job applications.

Expedition U.S.A.! is a program that involves learners in interpreting maps, charts, graphs, and text files. Information is supplied about natural and manufactured products, population trends, and gross state products for all of the regions of the United States. Regional data are provided for specific topics such as fruit production in the Southeast, Indian reservation lands in the Mountain West region, and tornado touchdowns in the North Central states. Readers must answer literal, inferential, and evaluative questions to complete a cross-country trek. While much information will undoubtedly be learned, the value of this program lies not in the facts acquired but in the involvement of the learners in locating information. They must first decide which sources are appropriate for each question and then use the information files and graphic aids to determine the answer. In addition to the questions in the program itself, the manual includes questions for group interaction, many of which will stimulate learners to think about the significance of information presented in graphic format. For example: For which North Central city did population decrease the most between 1970 and 1980? What economic developments contributed to this decline? Which region of the United States derives the largest percentage of its gross regional product from trade? From the service sector? From government? From agriculture? From manufacturing? Which region is the least agricultural? Which has the smallest service economy? Can you think of any reasons why these statistics might be as they are?

The *Geometric Supposer* series for mathematics engages learners in problem solving rather than merely getting right answers. With the programs in this series, the user constructs, labels, and measures a wide variety of geometric figures: points and lines, circles, quadrilaterals, and triangles. The programs are designed to engage users in analyzing, evaluating, collecting data, generalizing, and thinking creatively and logically. As they explore figures, they discover relationships and formulate and test conjectures.

Once again, the examples of software programs in this section are illustrative only. They have been briefly described in order to indicate that instructional software that involves thinking and problem solving is available. While it may take some time to locate good materials, it is far better that teachers spend time seeking worthwhile software than that learners spend time on meaningless routine practice with computer programs of low quality. If time for searching is unavailable, then perhaps a better alternative is simply to forget about purchasing and using packaged software and to concentrate instead on flexible uses of basic application tools such as word processors, databases, spreadsheets, and graphing programs.

SUMMARY: LITERACY IN A TECHNOLOGICAL AGE

Technology is advancing rapidly and finding its way into many phases of personal, business, industrial, and social life. To be literate today, both teachers and learners must be comfortable with technology. By using computers as an integral part of adult literacy programs, they will experience functional applications of one type of technology, which should help them feel more comfortable with the changes they are facing in the world about them.

Many possibilities for using word processors, databases, spreadsheets, graphing programs, selected software for comprehension and vocabulary practice, interactive text adventures, and simulations have been suggested in this chapter. The ideas might be overwhelming to people who have had limited experience with computers. The best advice is to start slowly by choosing just one type of software that seems most meaningful and useful for the situation. Several sessions of fun with a crossword maker or a poster-printing program are not wasted if they create a feeling of excitement and power over the computer. Using just the basic features of a word processor might be the next step. But wherever one starts, the important thing is to begin taking steps now so today's learners will have literacy with both books and other forms of information storage and retrieval.

« 6 »

Staff Selection and Development

As provisions for lifelong learning become more prevalent in the community and the workplace, teachers who are specifically prepared as adult educators will be in demand. The use of part-time staff members from unrelated disciplines will diminish. Adult education will become a full-time profession rather than a way to supplement one's income.

The facilitation of adult learning as a dynamic, interactive process requires teachers with particular personal and professional qualities. The qualities include, but go beyond, academic preparation. Knowledge of the subject matter for an adult education course, while necessary, is not sufficient; in addition, teachers must have an understanding of adult learning theory along with the insights and ability to apply principles derived from that theory. Teachers must recognize and respect the vast personal living experience and work knowledge that adults bring to the learning situation and must be able to build curricula around those backgrounds and interests. They must also be sensitive to the feelings that adults have about schools, about themselves as learners, and about their competence in reading, writing, math, technology, and learning in general. Teachers must be skilled in communications and decision making, not only to be effective instructors but also to carry out such essential activities as public relations, marketing, budgeting, and proposal writing.

The purposes of this chapter are to elaborate on the qualities for adult educators, provide guidelines for selecting personnel, and offer suggestions for maintaining and enhancing professional expertise. The personal and professional qualities to be sought are described in the first section, and suggestions are included for locating and interviewing potential staff members. In the second section, staff development activities are described. Suggestions for teacher evaluation are provided in the third section. Finally, since volunteers serve as tutors in a large number of programs, recommendations are made for preparing them to work with adults.

TEACHER SELECTION

A person with a strong academic background and professional preparation for teaching might or might not function well with adult learners. Teachers must be sought who have personal and professional traits that are necessary for implementing a whole language philosophy with older learners. Although personal and professional characteristics overlap, they are differentiated below for the purpose of explaining them and justifying their inclusion. Personal qualities include general knowledge, sensitivity to people, and good communication skills. Professional qualities include a philosophy about adult education, the ability to translate that philosophy and knowledge into practice, and organizational and managerial skills.

Personal Qualities

A teacher who will be working with people from diverse cultural and educational backgrounds must be aware of and interested in the many issues, topics, and concerns that are important to adults. This does not mean that the teacher must have a great depth of knowledge about a multitude of subjects; rather, he or she should have enough awareness to recognize timely information that is significant to learners. Teachers who are knowledgeable about and involved in political, social, and economic activities are continually expanding their views of how the world works. With the broad general knowledge attained through such involvement, they will feel comfortable using current topics and issues as the focus for lessons centered on authentic content in a realistic context. They will be confident in designing lessons in which reading and writing are used as tools for achieving greater understandings about the world rather than lessons in which reading and writing skills are seen as separate content to be taught. Knowledgeable teachers will bring a multitude of diverse resources to the learning situation and will introduce content that links with the learners' prior experiences.

Perhaps more important, teachers who have broad general backgrounds and are actively involved in a range of community activities will be sensitive to divergent beliefs, values, and opinions of learners. Brookfield (1986a) contends that one of the significant tasks of adult educators is ". . . to nurture in them [individuals' minds] a healthy skepticism toward ideologically biased explanations of the world" (p. 151). To accomplish this, teachers must create an educational setting where diversity is valued and respected, where ". . . beliefs, values, and notions are externalized and subjected to collaborative analysis and in which participants are always ready to alter their lines of inquiry on the basis of newly realized insights or interests" (Brookfield, 1986b, p. 217). Variations in learners' views are often related to cultural, ethical, and political backgrounds. The teacher must be receptive to the divergent views that will surface and must be capable of guiding lessons so that differences are recognized and explored, not argued or condemned. An adult educator must indeed be sensitive, responsive, and nonjudgmental.

The feelings that a teacher has about diversity in learners extend to their language abilities as well as their beliefs and opinions about worldly matters. Actually, it is in the realm of language where attitudes toward adult learners often appear. During the selection process, when potential teachers are asked about their reasons for choosing to work with adults, they should be prodded to look inward toward their real reasons for applying for the position. If the prodding leads to expressions of negative attitudes and ideas—for instance, that adults with limited language competence or different language patterns have limited learning capacities— then the interviewer might have a legitimate concern about a person's contributions to an adult literacy program. Negative attitudes and false assumptions are difficult to overcome, and they are sensed by the learners perhaps more readily than they are consciously recognized by the teacher. Teachers who hold such views may have limited influence on learners' academic successes and improved self-concepts. A person who consciously or unconsciously sees teaching primarily as a forum for improving others' deficient skills or for providing them the "right facts" should be discouraged from working in an adult literacy program. A teacher who assumes a role of presenting information in a didactic way with a goal of getting the right answer from learners is not effective with adults. A more appropriate perception of the teaching role is that of building lessons upon the learners' knowledge and experiences and helping them acquire the tools for lifelong learning.

Because communication is essential for learning and teaching, teachers in whole language programs must be proficient with language. They should be attentive listeners, articulate speakers, regular readers, and thoughtful writers. They must feel confident with all elements of language so that they will communicate effectively, present good models for learners, and see no need to use prepackaged skills lessons to compensate for their insecurity about language. Their language abilities can be assessed during carefully planned interviews that include both oral and written components. Using questions such as those in Figure 6.1, the interviewer will have an opportunity to note candidates' listening and speaking abilities as well as gain insights about their personal qualities and beliefs about adult education.

For additional insights about their language abilities, candidates can be asked to complete some writing as a part of the interview. They might be asked to choose from among two or three topics and write at least 200 words about their selection. The proposed topics can be ones that will elicit feelings about education and teaching, such as "What do you consider your most valuable educational or learning experience?" or "Why do you think you would be a successful teacher with adults?"

In addition to giving candidates an opportunity to exhibit their communication skills, clearly many of the questions in the written and oral parts of the interviews are designed to elicit attitudes and beliefs about the place of language in the learning process. The interviewer should get some good indications as to whether the candidate believes that reading and writing are processes that facilitate learning rather than subjects to be mastered, that listening and speaking are essential correlates of reading and writing, and that the language of the learner is valid and respectable.

Professional Qualities

While it may be easy to state opinions, effective teachers in a whole language program should be able to support their beliefs with insights gained from sound theory and research. Some of the interview questions in Figure 6.1 are designed to enable the reviewer to determine whether potential teachers are aware of the implications of recent research in psycholinguistics, sociolinguistics, and cognition. Research from these disciplines gives credence to the role of language as the medium by which people participate in society and learn more about the world. If teachers are to participate in a program based on a whole language philosophy, they must

FIGURE 6.1   Guidelines for Oral Interview of Staff

1. What kinds of teaching experience have you had with reading, writing, English, math, computers?
2. Are you teaching now? Would it be possible for me to observe your class?
3. What does whole language teaching mean to you? What do you know about the writing process?
4. What does the definition of reading as an interactive process mean to you?
5. How is questioning related to instruction?
6. What group experiences have you had as a learner or a teacher? What are some important responsible behaviors for a group member?
7. Why would small group teaching be a good arrangement for teaching adults?
8. With what kinds of professional decision-making experiences have you been involved? What was your role? What was the outcome?
9. What kinds of community involvement have you had?
10. How much reading do you do? What kinds?
11. What professional journals do you read regularly? What conferences have you attended recently?
12. What part of the job announcement attracted you? What do you think you need to be able to fill the requirements of this position?
13. What do you consider your strengths? What do you have to offer to this position?
14. What do you consider your weaknesses? What kinds of difficulties do you anticipate?
15. How do you feel about keeping records? Are you conscientious in doing so?
16. How do you feel about regular attendance by learners in an adult education program? What can a teacher do about this?
17. What expertise and experience do you have in advising or counseling adults?
18. How do you feel about working with different kinds of people who have some ownership in this program: union leaders, management personnel, school administrators, community resource people?
19. What do you hope to be doing ten years from now? How are language and language learning involved in your career plans in adult education? What other areas do you plan to pursue?

understand the importance of communication and interaction as a two-way process in which both learners and teachers are engaged. Indeed, human interaction is a thread that runs through our daily lives; its significance is dependent on the kind of communication that takes place in each encounter, whether it is a weight loss group, an alcoholics support program, or continuing education. "Through communication members of groups reach some understanding of one another, build trust, coordinate their actions, plan strategies for a goal accomplishment, agree upon a division of labor, conduct all group activity . . ." (Johnson & Johnson, 1987, p. 173). Through language, adults become active participants in learning rather than passive recipients of information.

The potential adult educator should also be familiar with recent research about the reading process, the writing process, adult learning, and their interrelationships. Furthermore, adult educators must be willing and able to apply the principles to instruction. Their efforts at translating theory into practice should form the basis for ongoing investigations, so that not only does research inform practice but practice informs research. Teachers who are familiar with the various factors that influence teaching and learning will implement what seems appropriate, question what does and does not work, and revise methods, materials, or techniques that are promising. Teachers who are in touch with the research and developments in the field will try out new ideas as professional knowledge expands; furthermore, they can confidently support their instructional practices. As teachers continue their contacts and gain more insights, they become more selective in the practices they choose. In addition, through their own involvement in learning, they better understand how one comes to know what is worth knowing; this involvement "frequently results in startling discoveries" about where learning originates and about the process of learning (Postman & Weingartner, 1969, p. 205). These startling discoveries are not just one-shot final answers but are steps toward an ever-deepening understanding of the learning process.

Because of the need for continuing professional development, teachers should be selected who are alert to new information and open to change. They should indicate that they have taken and will continue to take advantage of numerous avenues for professional development, such as academic course work, informal study groups, professional meetings and conferences, regular professional reading, and dialogues with other practitioners and recognized leaders in the field. Teachers should also be willing to take part in disseminating information. Making presentations at conferences and writing articles for professional publications are ways of sharing insights with others; preparing for presentations and articles helps one think through one's practices and their theoretical support.

In addition to knowledge about teaching, teachers of adults need organizational and managerial skills. When the teaching role is focused on facilitating learning rather than presenting information, the ability to organize a class to promote group activities and respond to individual needs within the group setting is essential. The facilitation of learning demands a different type of organizational skill than that required for lecturing or "giving" information. Teachers must be willing to create and maintain environments that are comfortable for learners and promote face-to-face interactions. Time-management and planning skills are necessary for designing lessons that will maintain students' active, ongoing participation. An organized teacher will be able to individualize during the lesson when members of the group are engaged in independent practice, whether reading, writing, or working at the computer. The teacher must be alert to indications of questions, problems, or boredom and must be able to shift from one learner to another to provide encouragement, ask a question that will prompt the person to take the next step, or assist with the revision of writing.

Beyond the responsibilities for instruction, teachers must keep accurate attendance records and regularly collect, file, and update materials. Many teachers in adult education programs will also be involved in recruiting students, marketing courses, and interacting with noneducation professionals. Suggestions for these aspects of the adult literacy program are offered in Chapter 7, but are mentioned here to emphasize the point that the interviewer should look for clues that the applicant is an organized person who is willing and able to undertake responsibilities beyond teaching.

Finding the Right People

In order to reach all potential applicants, announcements for positions might be posted in university placement offices, in local newspapers, on university bulletin boards, and in sites where adult education programs are offered. The postings should indicate the subject matter expertise required as well as the teaching background expected. In business and industrial settings, teacher certification might not be necessary, but in GED programs and community education courses it is typically required. Perhaps as adult education becomes more prevalent, certification especially for this field will be instituted.

Advertising for a teacher of adults is the easy part. Finding the right person is more challenging. Once the applications begin to arrive, how can the selection be made? While some indications of a prospective teacher's background can be gained from the paperwork—a letter of application, vita, academic transcript, and letters of recommendation—the most revealing insights will come during a well-planned interview. Oral and written interviews, as described earlier, provide a framework for both the interviewer and the candidate to assess the person's qualifications for the position.

STAFF DEVELOPMENT

Although the description of a career adult educator may paint a picture of a paragon who devotes endless time and energy to the job, the portrayal is really that of a well-rounded person who is interested in and sensitive to others and who is up-to-date regarding adult education and world events. Such qualities are always in the process of development and refinement. Much change will occur as a result of one's daily self-evaluation of teaching as well as through participating in informal and planned staff development activities.

With the expansion of lifelong learning opportunities, an adult literacy teacher need not be a loner once the teaching begins. Many opportunities will be available to continue one's professional growth in concert with others in the field. When teachers join together for professional activities, significant growth and personal satisfaction are forthcoming. Many literacy programs in community centers, worksites, and libraries involve several staff members; whenever more than one teacher is engaged in adult education in a given situation, the staff members can and should function as a team for purposes of professional growth. An adult educator working alone must look harder for opportunities to share and learn with peers, but should make every effort to find others in similar circumstances who might meet regularly for support and professional growth activities.

Benefits of a Common Outlook

Staff members who share common beliefs about teaching and learning work better together. They are in general agreement about what the teachers and learners hope to achieve, the teaching and learning strategies to be used, and the outcomes to be accomplished. Planning and teaching are focused on shared goals and objectives. This is not to say that everyone will be alike. Teachers have different personalities and they implement a theory in unique ways. Differences among staff members are respected, just as they are among learners. Nonetheless, there is a common thread of belief that gives coherence and unity to the program and provides support and cohesiveness for the staff and consistency for the learners.

A common outlook is preserved by careful selection of teachers who are committed to adult literacy and the philosophy of the program. Even with careful selection, however, teachers might be hired who seem in the interview to support the philosophy but need assistance in implementing it. Also, teachers who have been working in the program may need to become familiar with current research and practice in order to update their backgrounds and teaching strategies. Whatever the commonalities and differences, ongoing staff development activities are important for nurturing and strengthening the program.

Staff Meetings for Professional Growth

Regularly scheduled staff meetings provide continuous opportunities for teachers to reassess their practices and exchange ideas and insights about changes in curriculum, methods, and materials. Staff meetings also provide a setting for resolving conflicts, solving problems, and determining long-range plans. The values of group interaction are as important for teachers as for adult learners. In a group, teachers can support one another and build on one another's ideas in order to strengthen themselves and the program. Indeed, the values are so great that it is imperative to have regular staff meetings devoted solely to professional growth.

What might occur in a staff development meeting? The sessions should parallel the kinds of learning environments and interactions the teachers are expected to practice with their students. Staff members might participate in reading, writing, discussing, and using the strategies they will incorporate in their lessons. The content might include such topics as questioning, brainstorming, or selecting and using materials. Suggestions for staff development sessions based on each of these three topics are given below.

The following scenario illustrates an inservice meeting about questioning, in which the questioning technique is both the content and the methodology for the session.

An Illustrative Scenario on Questioning.   The group leader for the day (program director or one of the teachers) has prepared a session on questioning techniques. The goal is that the teachers will evaluate their questioning techniques and develop a set of guidelines for questioning. The leader will model questioning techniques as an integral part of the session. An article (such as Ornstein, 1987) will be used for reference.

Introducing the session, the leader indicates that the focus will be on the art of questioning. A quote from Brookfield (1986b) is read: "Facilitators of learning see themselves as resources for learning, rather than as didactic instructors who have all the answers. They stress that they are engaged in a democratic, student-centered enhancement of individual learning and that responsibility for setting the direction and methods of learning rests as much with the learner as with the educator" (p. 63). To activate the teachers' background knowledge, the leader asks: What does that quote have to do with questioning? How do you feel when teachers ask you questions? Why is questioning considered an art? In what ways have you used questioning successfully? What problems have you experienced when you have raised questions with your adult learners? What questions do you have about questioning? The leaders allows appropriate "wait time" for responses and withholds all judgments and answers in order to create an environment in which the teachers (learners now) will find their own solutions.

With their questions to guide them, the teachers read silently an article on the topic. Following the reading, they discuss such questions as: In what ways did the author confirm what you believe? Which of your questions were answered? What new insights about questioning did you get? What other questions do you now have about questioning?

The teachers are invited to evaluate the leader's use of the principles of questioning during the session. Perhaps the teachers will recognize that all answers were accepted nonjudgmentally— no single "right" answer was expected. This realization is as important for teachers as it is for their adult learners; teachers are often more comfortable in their teacher role of asking questions than they are in the learner's role, and it is helpful for them to re-experience and think about their feelings as group participants among peers. The teachers might realize that the leader handled responses in a positive manner, encouraged each person to contribute, and accepted comments that were in conflict with other ideas or with the text. Since it might not be obvious to the teachers, the leader could mention a moment when he or she picked up a body language clue about a willingness or reticence to respond.

To conclude the session, the staff members might work in pairs to compile lists of guidelines about questioning to use in their lessons.

A Staff Meeting on Brainstorming. Brainstorming is another topic for an inservice session. Brainstorming is a more effective way to activate prior knowledge than introducing a topic by simply writing it on the board or announcing it to the class. Using a brainstorming technique to get the group involved in the topic of brainstorming, the staff members could be asked to think of all the ways they know to help learners link information the learners already have to the content of an upcoming lesson. As their ideas are listed on the board, the teachers will probably realize that they know a lot more than they thought. To stimulate further thinking, they can be asked: Why are these strategies for introducing topics so beneficial? Following this activation of their knowledge, the teachers might read an article (such as Bransford and Johnson, 1972) that presents evidence in support of the fact that learning and retention are increased when new information is linked with prior knowledge. After reading the article silently, the teachers can evaluate their brainstorming list to determine the extent to which their prior knowledge was relevant. They can add new ideas to their list of ways of activating background knowledge and, finally, evaluate how their use of brainstorming in this session proved useful to them.

A Staff Meeting on Materials. Staff development meetings might be devoted to helping teachers make informed choices about materials to use. Teachers need to become familiar with a varied collection of appropriate materials so that they will be better able to select and create their own. In preparation for an inservice program, the person conducting the session might collect a variety of materials that are suitable for adult learners. The materials should contain meaningful information related to the learners' work or personal lives, be selected on the basis of their high-interest adult content rather than on the basis of a reading level, expose learners to alternative viewpoints and previously unexplored subjects, and be provocative (Kazemek & Rigg, 1985b). A variety of media can be used, including films, poetry, pamphlets, objects, music, pictures, technical materials, cartoons, graphs, computer programs, and learner-generated materials.

The staff members, working in pairs, can select an item and develop a plan for the application of whole language strategies for using the material with adult learners. The sample lessons in Chapters 2 and 3 might serve as prototypes for the planning of whole language activities around the material selected. After a timed period, their ideas can be shared with the group for critiquing and extending. Sharing in this way provides momentum for teachers to look at realistic and appropriate alternatives to workbooks. A session of this type can easily be repeated, having teachers select different materials the next time. A third session might even be held, in which the teachers bring in materials that they have selected to fit the criteria.

Other Topics for Staff Meetings. The range of possibilities for inservice programs devoted to instruction is endless. Topics could include revising, editing, clustering, mapping, using story grammar to guide reading and writing, managing individual differences in a group setting, developing word meanings (vocabulary), recognizing types of text structures in science and social studies materials, analyzing oral reading behaviors, and writing personalized math problems.

Staff members might engage in inservice activities to gain facility with computers. Because word processing can contribute to an adult literacy program in many ways and because it is also a meaningful way to get acquainted with the computer, a series of meetings might be devoted to learning to use it. Learning to use a word processor should be accomplished in hands-on guided practice sessions, which could be replicas of the sessions described in Chapter 4 on the computer awareness course.

Staff meetings can also be forums for the sharing of new ideas and insights that individuals gain from other types of professional experiences. Teachers might demonstrate or summarize information and ideas gained from formal courses and from local, state, and national meetings and conferences they have attended. Professional adult educators also keep abreast of current developments through journals such as those listed in Appendix C. Information can be shared by circulating the journals, perhaps with asterisks, highlighting, or marginal notes on specific pages or articles that would be of interest to others.

TEACHER EVALUATION

Good teachers evaluate their lessons every day; they consider how the students responded, what went well, and what might be changed next time. More comprehensive periodic evaluations, carried out cooperatively with the project director, provide opportunities to look at the curriculum and instruction from a broader perspective.

Because the director is responsible for the quality of the program, he or she must be knowledgeable about the curriculum and the theory that supports it. Whether in a community center, public school community education center, or worksite, a program for adults must be overseen by a director who has internalized the theory and who understands how it is reflected in practice. Preferably the director is one who has been, or still is, directly engaged in instructing adults within a whole language framework. Managerial skills, while important, are not sufficient. A successful adult literacy program must be managed well, of course, but it will be truly successful only when evaluation is based on the same theoretical foundation on which the program has been developed.

Much informal evaluation will be carried out by the teachers and program director during casual daily contacts. A director who takes the title literally and directs from a central office, but who rarely interacts with staff or learners, can have little sensitivity to the daily flow of the program and to the accomplishments of learners and staff.

An effective program director also interacts with the total staff on a weekly basis. This may be a short group meeting to remind people of special events, identify needs, or solve a minor problem. It may be a session to work cooperatively on publicity, recruiting, awards ceremonies, and other tasks such as described in Chapter 7. It may be a staff development program as described in this chapter. In addition to providing opportunities for work on necessary tasks and for inservice activities, these weekly group meetings inevitably involve the director and the staff in ongoing evaluations of the program.

Of course, more formal evaluations will be carried out, too. The program director will meet each staff member individually to discuss together six important areas: personal attributes, organizational skills, involvement with the project, relationships with colleagues, relationships with students, and teaching effectiveness. While some of those areas can be assessed through daily and weekly contacts, the director's comments about relationships with students and teaching effectiveness can be valid only when each teacher has been observed for a total class period on several separate occasions.

Evaluation is a way to celebrate successes as well as a means to foster continued growth and improvement. Teachers who evaluate themselves and who are evaluated in this spirit of continued growth and development will evaluate learners in the same spirit.

RECRUITMENT AND PREPARATION OF TUTORS

Along with full-time professionals, individual tutors will be a continuing need. In some locales literacy programs are limited in scope and size so that classes given by qualified teachers are not available. In addition, even within a comprehensive program of offerings, some adults may still need individual help, particularly in the areas of reading and writing.

Locating Volunteers

Volunteers are available in many communities, but they must be recruited and prepared for working with adults. An active recruitment program, using a variety of media and personal contacts, is needed to capture the interest of potential tutors. An aggressive campaign can be launched by contacting many organizations and requesting permission to make presentations, display posters, and distribute informational flyers. Church, neighborhood, and parent groups; community and college service organizations; ethnic clubs; and university departments (sociology, guidance and counseling, education) are excellent places to begin the quest for tutors. Personal presentations at these organizations are especially valuable, particularly when a local literacy program is just starting and is, therefore, relatively unknown. Recruitment posters can be displayed in libraries, universities, stores, markets, employment agencies, military recruitment offices, and social service agencies throughout the community. Ads can be placed in daily and weekly newspapers and church newsletters. Announcements can be broadcast on local radio stations. The announcements should include assurances that potential volunteers will receive guidance in working with adult learners.

Preparing Tutors

Volunteers are expected to participate in a series of sessions to prepare them to tutor. Several organizational matters must receive attention in arranging these sessions. When people show interest in tutoring, their names, addresses, and phone numbers should be obtained so that personal letters and an agenda can be sent about two weeks before the sessions begin. Usually it is desirable to have about twice as many registrations as desired for the preparation sessions in order to get enough tutors. Ten to twelve persons make a good group; the limit for the preparation sessions should be twenty. Early evenings, 5:30 to 7:30, are the favored times for meetings, especially for the many volunteers who are working women, but other times may work well with particular populations. Ideally, the sessions will be carried out in the center where volunteers will work so that they become familiar with the facilities. Tutoring at home, with neither support nor supervision, is not advocated. Serving coffee, tea, and cookies creates a pleasant ambience and helps relax volunteers who come with the apprehensions that often accompany a new situation.

The content and methodology of a preparation program for tutors must be carefully planned. While tutors cannot be expected to become as knowledgeable about teaching as adult educators who have prepared specifically for the field, they can learn to implement whole language principles. To acquaint volunteers with the philosophy, procedures, and practices of the program, a series of six two-hour sessions is recommended. The following suggestions for content are based on the assumption that volunteers will tutor primarily in reading and writing, but the general format can be adapted to other areas, such as GED and computer courses, as well.

The first session will, of course, be devoted to an overview of the program and its purposes. Volunteers can become acquainted with one another and share their reasons for wanting to participate. Activities can be planned to sensitize them to the characteristics, feelings, and needs of adult learners. The reasons for an adult literacy program in the particular local setting at the present time can be explained. Simulations and exercises can be carried out to help volunteers understand the rationale for using a whole language philosophy, that is, to provide meaningful real-world content and build upon the strengths that adults bring to the learning situation.

The second session might focus on current insights about language and learning. This is especially important since many tutors may have little or no knowledge of recent research about language processes and their implications for adults. Without guidance, tutors will be apt to implement teaching practices that are unsupported by new professional insights and will be tempted to use outmoded packaged materials without realizing that more effective alternatives are possible. Therefore, attention must be given to such questions as: What is a whole language philosophy and how can it be translated into action? What are the implications of the definition of reading as an interactive, constructive, dynamic process? How should knowledge about the writing process influence teaching and learning? How do listening and speaking relate to learning and teaching?

In the third session, instructional strategies might be modeled. An actual demonstration of a whole language lesson would be a very effective way of illustrating how the principles of a whole language philosophy are put into action. Secure, enthusiastic adult learners who are enrolled in the local program might be willing to role play a lesson and offer comments on their reactions to the approaches being used. This presentation could be followed by a discussion of the techniques and by lesson simulations in which pairs of volunteers role play the tutor and the learner.

Since instructional strategies are crucial to the success of the program, the fourth session might continue to focus on them. While the previous session had an adult learner as a resource person, perhaps this one could feature a local adult teacher as a consultant to provide examples and demonstrate strategies that have have been used successfully. The teacher's examples might include suggestions for helping adults learn vocabulary, spelling, and grammar in purposeful ways. Part of this session might also be spent on the selection and use of materials that are appropriate and effective for adults.

In the fifth session, volunteers might be introduced to the role of technology, particularly computers, in literacy efforts. They should be guided to consider how technology is related to the lives of adults in society, the workplace, and education. Hands-on activities with computers would probably take up the major part of this meeting. If the participants have little experience with computers, attention might be centered on the word processor, the most versatile and useful tool for a whole language program. A few basic features of word processing might be introduced. These features should be incorporated in activities that model and simulate the use of word processing to create and edit materials within a tutoring situation. If time permits, one or two other appropriate software programs could be modeled, for example, a crossword puzzle maker or a program providing practice with cloze passages created from the learner's own text.

Assessment and record keeping might be the focus of the final session. The tutors should understand that assessment is much broader than testing and that traditional measures that yield grade level scores are demeaning to adults and inconsistent with the goals of a whole language program. Alternative means of assessment must be discussed, including portfolios of writings, personal anecdotes, observations, and checklists. The tutors should know what kinds of records are kept and how the learner and the tutor are involved in their development and maintenance. Because this is the last session, some time must be reserved to deal with such questions as: Where and when do we begin? With whom? What triggers can be used to get started? Where can we get support and help when needed?

While the content of the tutor preparation sessions is important, the methodology is even more so. The meetings should be conducted in the same dynamic, interactive manner that the volunteers will be expected to use with adult learners. Each session might start with 10 minutes of uninterrupted sustained silent reading by the volunteers and their instructor. In order that this can start at the first meeting, the letter to volunteers announcing the preparation should alert them to bring a book to read. An effective way to help volunteers see the value of this silent reading time is to delay explanation of uninterrupted sustained silent reading until the last session, at which time everyone shares their feelings about the purpose and value of a planned quiet reading time, even during a relatively short class period.

The rationale for a whole language program must be experienced through appropriate listening, speaking, and writing activities. Group members can participate in 10 minutes of free writing each session so that they better understand the purpose of having adult learners write. Teaching and learning strategies can be modeled, and research articles that support particular practices can be read and discussed at appropriate times. Experiential situations can be created in which volunteers are guided to assess their feelings about teaching adults, investigate possible reasons for a learner's lack of motivation, or realize the values of clustering as preparation for writing. The goal is for tutors to experience the self-directed learning and thinking that they, in turn, will nurture in the adults with whom they will work.

Supervising and Supporting Volunteers

Supervision and support are extremely important. Rare is the person who learns something new and then immediately practices it perfectly. Once tutoring begins, the program director or supervisor should be available to answer questions and make suggestions. In addition, observations of lessons should be seen as opportunities to promote further growth. The first observation might occur after a tutor and learner have been together three or four times, with the purpose of early identification of the tutor's ability to use the strategies taught during the preparation program. After a session has been observed, the supervisor and tutor might review the lesson, perhaps focusing on the writing phase and discussing such questions as: Did the learner complete a story? Did you have the learner tell the story before writing it? Did you read the story back to the learner, asking him or her to listen to see whether it was right? Did you ask the student if he or she wanted to make changes? What did you learn about the learner's interests? Did you and the learner complete the record-keeping forms? Do you need any materials? What positive feelings do you have about the session? Do you have other feelings about the session you'd like to share?

Of course, periodic observations should continue, both as a means of maintaining support and as a way of showing that the contributions of tutors are important to the program. Other types of recognition for tutors' efforts must also be given high priority. Appreciation can be expressed informally by brief comments, a smile, a hug, or a phone call. At regular intervals, a letter can be sent to confirm the continuing appreciation for volunteer efforts. An article in the project's newsletter is likewise rewarding to most tutors and might inspire others to volunteer. During awards ceremonies for learners, tutors might also receive certificates and gifts such as books or notepads and pens.

Because volunteers donate their time and energy, they may find it necessary to stop tutoring. When this happens, an exit interview can provide valuable information about the provisions for tutors as well as about the quality of the program. Responses to the following questions can be very helpful: Why did you come to this program? Did the program help you reach your goal? What do you like best about this program? What do you like least? What suggestions do you have for improving the program? Do you plan to return some time in the future? Why are you leaving?

SUMMARY: TEAM BUILDING

No matter how good the philosophy and how much research supports it, an effective educational program depends on qualified, sensitive teachers. The first requisite for an adult literacy program is to locate and select good staff members. Those good teachers become even better as they have informal contacts with their co-workers, participate in well-planned staff development activities, and keep abreast of new developments in the field by reading journals, attending conferences, and building networks with professionals beyond the local area.

Of course, contacts with other staff members in the program will be most important because they offer daily support, encouragement, and stimulation. The more the staff shares a common view about teaching and learning, the more valuable those contacts are. The more teachers work together and engage in informal and planned staff development, the more they share a common view. The team that is built continues to grow and perpetuate a winning program in which the ultimate goal of benefiting the learners is reached.

≪ 7 ≫
Program Development and Management

How is an adult literacy program developed? Is it truly a program planned as a whole or is it characterized as a series of classes offered because they seem to be needed and instructors are available? If a coherent planned program exists, should it continue in its present form or might revisions be desirable? Whether services are already being provided or a new program is being planned, the program ought to have clearly defined goals, be based on a framework supported by research, and be designed and managed in ways that indicate respect for adult learners. It should be housed in appropriate facilities and should also include plans for publicity and recruitment efforts to reach its intended audience. Teachers need to be aware of, or better yet involved in, all aspects of program planning, operation, and evaluation. Because the evaluation of the program as a whole is closely related to the evaluation of learner growth, special consideration must be given to ways to assess the accomplishments of adults—ways that are not carryovers from traditional testing procedures and grade level designations.

The first part of this chapter raises questions to be considered when developing adult literacy programs, evaluating those already in existence, or writing proposals to secure approval and funding. How do the goals of the program reflect the needs and purposes of the intended learners and their supporters? What views does the overall program represent in theory and in practice? What phases of the program need development or revision? How can all the pieces be pulled together into a unified whole? What physical facilities are desirable and where should they be located? What should be considered in planning a budget?

The second part of the chapter includes suggestions for publicizing the program. Publicity and public relations are important during the development of a program and throughout its existence. The general public needs to know about the program for several reasons. Knowledgeable people in the community or the work-place may provide moral support to the staff and learners. Perhaps they will recommend the program to adults who might benefit from it. They might become volunteer tutors. They are often in positions where they can influence decisions about whether such programs should be offered and how they should be financed. From another perspective, publicity is needed to celebrate the successes of the program; recognize the efforts of learners, teachers, and tutors; and promote the idea that lifelong learning is a viable and valuable undertaking for all people.

Recruitment of learners is given attention in the third part of the chapter, and recognition activities are described in the fourth section. Many potential learners are reluctant to enroll in adult education programs. A number of techniques can be used to alert them to the services that are available and to help them realize that this experience will be different from their often painful memories of school. They need encouragement to take that first very difficult step in admitting the need for help and perhaps the even more difficult step of actually beginning a class. While the intrinsic rewards that come with success and the excitement of learning are incomparable, public recognition is also important; therefore, suggestions for recognition ceremonies and awards are included as well.

Finally, issues concerning assessment will be presented and suggestions for evaluation of adult learners will be offered. Assessment is much broader than testing (Farr & Carey, 1986; Goodman, Goodman, & Hood, 1989; Valencia & Pearson, 1987). Traditional testing, especially in reading, writing, and mathematics, is product-oriented rather than process-oriented. Paper-and-pencil tests do not measure growth toward the goal of learning to learn. Furthermore, grade level scores are totally inappropriate for measuring growth in the learning process at all ages, and especially with adults. Alternative means of assessing progress will be described, with indications of ways in which to involve learners in the evaluation process. Recommended procedures include portfolios of work, anecdotal records, checklists, and questionnaires.

PROGRAM PLANNING AND EVALUATION

Program planning and evaluation go hand in hand. The offerings in established community education programs and other adult learning centers should be evaluated regularly. Whether the administrators and teachers believe that "everything is fine" or, preferably, that "there is always room for improvement," program evaluation is essential. Efforts should be made to determine whether a master plan with a consistent framework is in place or whether the program is a smattering of offerings that have grown topsy-turvy simply because funds were available and teachers could be found who were willing to try their hand at an adult education course. The purpose of the evaluation is not to pinpoint blame for problems but to lead to planning for a more effective program. One of the marks of a good adult literacy program is that it is under constant planning, evaluation, and change.

The Program Framework

As adult literacy spreads, more and more programs are being started in community centers, correctional institutions, and the workplace. In these cases, planning must start from the ground up, which can be an advantage in that firmly entrenched practices need not be challenged. Initiatives for new programs might come from plant or prison educational advisors, librarians, community service agency representatives, labor leaders, management personnel, or adult educators who believe that more comprehensive and cohesive lifelong learning programs should be established in a given area. Regardless of the origin, it is imperative that the planners identify the goals and outcomes, investigate the need, justify the philosophy and describe related instructional implications, outline the program organization, and project the funding needs. Consideration must also be given to locating adequate space, gathering materials, and selecting and preparing teachers and tutors.

In most cases, a written proposal is needed, either to gain approval of the board of directors, union representatives, and management personnel or to seek funding from a federal, state, or charitable organization. The proposal should be clear and concise. It must outline the overall program as well as present specific personnel and financial requirements to be provided by the sponsoring organization. The assumption is that a team consisting of adult educators and personnel from the organization will work together, first to informally explore initial interest in the project and then to write a formal proposal. State and federal agencies, charitable foundations, and the larger business and industrial organizations usually have their own forms or lists of guidelines for information that must be provided in a proposal.

Questions to Guide Planning and Evaluation

Whether evaluating an ongoing program or developing a proposal for a sponsoring organization or funding agency, the following questions should be addressed:

1. *Purposes.* What are the overall goals, specific purposes, and scope of the program? What outcomes are expected? Is the focus on literacy at lower competency levels only, or is attention also given to expanding reading and writing abilities at all levels, including study skills, test-taking, and technical writing? Are GED classes offered? Are computer awareness classes provided and/or are computers integrated within reading and writing classes?

2. *Need.* Why is the program needed at this time and place? How does it serve the needs of the people, the organization, the community, and society?

3. *Audience.* Who is served by the program? Who is eligible? How much interest is there among those eligible? How are participants reached and recruited, especially those who are eligible but not particularly motivated? What efforts are made to reach minorities, women, the unemployed, and people who speak other languages? What costs, if any, are participants expected to pay? What financial aid is available if participants must pay?

4. *Theoretical foundations.* Upon what theory and adult-oriented research is the instructional program based? What types of reading, writing, and instructional strategies are consistent with that theory and research? How does instruction for GED reflect consistency with current emphases on learning how to learn rather than on remembering information? How are computer classes organized to promote independent learning and transfer of skills to other technology? How is technology used to enhance the core of the instructional program?

5. *Instructors.* Who are the instructors? What qualifications do they have for teaching adults? What background do they have in reading and writing processes? What preparation is available for this particular project? What plans are there for inservice activities to evaluate the program and update the staff?

6. *Class organization.* When, where, and for how long is instruction offered? Is instruction offered to individuals or to classes? If classes, what are the minimum and maximum class sizes?

What is the impact of class size on group interactions? For whom and for how long is individual tutoring available? What efforts are made to adjust class times and course lengths to learners' needs?

7. *Physical environment.* What physical facilities, materials, and equipment are needed? How do they reflect consideration of and respect for adult learners? To what extent are they available at this site?

8. *Recognition.* How are the accomplishments of learners recognized? What kinds of recognition and awards are given?

9. *Program evaluation.* How is the program evaluated? How often is evaluation carried out? What are valid indicators that the purposes are being fulfilled? What are the indications that the needs of the individuals, the community, and the organization are being met?

10. *Budget.* What financial commitment is needed to carry out the program in a worthwhile manner? What does the budget include and what is the rationale for each item?

Obviously some questions are of much greater significance than others. Questions dealing with purposes and theoretical foundations are harder to answer and may indicate areas in which changes are difficult to make. Perhaps because they are difficult, they are often given less attention than administrative and organizational matters. Nonetheless, they must be considered in depth as a basis for both initial planning and making changes to maintain a viable program. Suggestions for finding answers to many of these questions have been offered throughout the book.

Physical Facilities

The sponsor's belief in and support for the program is subtly—or not so subtly—indicated by the location, size, and features of the facility. Literacy programs can be provided in many locations: schools, colleges, storefront sites and shopping malls, manufacturing plants, business settings, and community service agencies. Obviously these sites, except for schools and colleges, are designed for purposes other than education, so locating suitable space within a building may not be easy.

Even in schools, the typical facilities might be inappropriate for adult learners. If classes are located in educational institutions, the instructional area should be carefully selected. Secondary classrooms are much more suitable than elementary classrooms. If the program must be offered in an elementary building, perhaps a teachers' lounge, library, cafeteria, or multi-purpose room could be used; a similar area might be preferred to a classroom in a secondary building as well. Because of the emotional feelings that many adults have about their earlier educational experiences, alternatives to elementary and secondary school buildings should be actively sought. Space might be found in a community college, university, YWCA, YMCA, or the conference room of a public library. Perhaps as lifelong learning gains more of a foothold, either facilities will be constructed in the community or special provisions will be made for multi-age teaching and learning activities within school buildings.

Programs in the workplace or in community service agencies should be housed in a central location accessible to the learners. While the location must be visible and easily found, it should also be "invisible" insofar as being identified as a place for remediation. In the workplace, employees might feel intimidated if they must walk to or through management areas for classes.

The name and sign for the facility should be chosen with care. Names such as "Reading Room," "Math Lab," or "Basic Education" create images of elementary school that are demeaning to adults. "Lifelong Learning Center" or "The Academy" are names that are more appropriate and acceptable to adults.

Wherever the facility is located, ample room should be available for small group instruction, tutorials, individual study, and secretarial work. Private areas for conferencing and testing are essential. The space must be large enough to include bookshelves, filing cabinets, and cupboards for display and storage of teaching and learning materials. If computer activities are to be integrated within reading, writing, and GED classes, the computers, printers, and software must be accommodated within the same area.

The physical surroundings must be warm, inviting, and furnished to convey a sense of respect for adult learners. Tables (round, if possible) and adult-sized chairs should be arranged to promote small group interactions. Paintings, mounted pictures or photos, and wall hangings representative of adult life should decorate the area. Clean curtains, functional blinds, and plants on windowsills or bookshelves help create a pleasant atmosphere. If computers are in the room, an erasable composition board should be used to eliminate chalk dust. The area should be filled with meaningful print: books, a dictionary, a thesaurus, a calendar, newspapers and clippings, magazines, maps, learners' writings—but no phonics charts. Writing paper and holders with pencils and markers can be placed in the centers of the tables. All of these aspects of the environment will lose their effect if the area is not organized, clean, and well-maintained. Without a doubt, a pleasant setting sends a clear message that learners are important and respected.

Money Matters

Budgets always present problems. Almost everyone believes that adult education is important, as long as it doesn't cost very much! But quality products and services do cost money. People don't really need gourmet foods and luxury cars, but neither should they be satisfied with a rice diet and riding bikes all the time. Often an education program, particularly for adults, is expected to hobble along on a rice and bike budget with minimal support. If a program is well-planned, well-executed, and based on sound theory, the results will reflect quality and the costs will be justified. An adequate budget for a quality program should be requested without apology. The exact figures will depend on the local situation, but the major costs will undoubtedly be for qualified teaching personnel. If a new program is being established, facilities, equipment, and materials will also be major items, but those costs should diminish in subsequent years. Included in the budget should be an allocation for recognition ceremonies and awards, an aspect for which funding is often omitted.

PUBLICITY

If literacy and lifelong learning are widely recognized as necessary today, why and for whom must adult education programs be publicized? What kinds of publicity programs will reach the people who need to know about them?

Audiences

Three major audiences should know about literacy programs:

1. The general public needs to be informed about literacy programs. Potential enrollees, as well as their friends and relatives, must know what services are available and how to make con-

tact. Potential tutors should be made aware of the opportunity to serve. The community as a whole, from which moral support is important and perhaps financial support is needed, should realize that local efforts are underway to respond to the need for a literate citizenry.

2. Business, industry, union, and other local leaders should understand that responsibilities for lifelong learning go beyond the community service and educational sectors. Those leaders should be inspired to support adult education programs and, perhaps, provide such opportunities in their organizations in order to enhance the quality of life in the workplace, in the community, and ultimately in society as a whole.

3. Program directors, teachers, sponsors, counselors, tutors, learners, and others who are or might be involved with adult education programs should be aware of alternatives to conventional approaches to teaching and learning. They should be challenged to evaluate approaches to see if they are truly adult-centered or merely adaptations of curricula and teaching approaches that are more appropriate for youngsters. Individuals involved with adult education should be cognizant that alternative teaching practices that respect the adult learner are possible and are supported by theory and research on reading, writing, and cognition.

The content for publicity efforts must be carefully planned, especially in light of the third purpose above—making people aware of qualitative differences in up-to-date adult education programs. Attention should be given to telling the *why* and *how* of the program rather than only the who, what, where, and when. The publicity strategies described below will serve several audiences and purposes simultaneously. In addition, many of the recruitment suggestions in the following section will publicize the program and at the same time encourage people to enroll.

Techniques

Adult education staff members who are engaged in community activities are natural ambassadors for the program. Through informal associations made by attending meetings, holding offices, and serving on community and professional committees, they will disseminate information and make contacts with community leaders who might suggest further contacts as well as promote the program themselves. Adult educators will develop relationships with leaders in businesses and industries who are in positions to encourage people to enroll, provide moral and financial support, and perhaps even establish on-site adult literacy programs.

Personal contacts are important, either as a follow-up to relationships formed through community activities or through special arrangements with key individuals. Staff members should be very sensitive to the use of personal contacts, however. While some people will respond to continual reminders, others are turned away by persistent, and what they might perceive as aggressive, overtures. Some people would rather get initial information through a flyer sent to the office than by a telephone call. Sometimes a secretary can be a good source of information about the best person to talk to and the most desirable way to contact that individual.

Regular communication channels—newspapers, radio, television, mail, and telephone—should be used as much as possible. Materials written by the adults in the program might be submitted for publication in local papers or magazines. Reporters might be called to do articles on the program's activities, the people enrolled, and special events. Radio and television producers might be contacted to arrange interviews with learners, teachers, and program sponsors. The staff must take the initiative rather than wait for media personnel to decide that the time is ripe for a feature story. Two or three special articles and interviews a year, preferably at times other than the typical media blitz on adult literacy in the fall, will help keep the program in the public eye.

Teachers who have experienced the rewards of teaching with a whole language framework are usually eager to share their successes with other educators, not necessarily to publicize a particular program but rather to promote an awareness of alternatives that might be of value to learners in general. Making presentations at professional conferences and writing articles for appropriate journals (such as listed in Appendix C) are excellent ways to help colleagues become aware of alternative approaches as well as to build a network for continued growth. Sometimes it is helpful to conduct local workshops for teachers and tutors who find it difficult to attend national meetings. Successful teachers might submit applications to teach courses at local colleges on teaching reading to adults. Short presentations might be made to preservice and in-service teacher education classes as a way to make professionals aware of adult literacy programs as well as secure some volunteer tutors (who might get credit for a pre-student teaching experience).

Another good way to publicize this type of program, especially the why and the how, is to invite observers to adult education classes. Better than observing, however, is to have guests become participant-observers. Labor leaders or business managers who are contemplating the establishment of adult literacy programs at their locations, and educators or potential tutors who want to see firsthand how a whole language philosophy is translated into action might benefit by becoming a part of a class and interacting with the learners and the teacher.

RECRUITMENT OF LEARNERS

Recruitment is a never-ending task that goes on day in and day out in an adult literacy program. Having a program is pointless unless it serves the people who need it most. While word about a good program will spread, efforts must be made to encourage those who do not hear the word or who hear but are fearful of embarking on yet another educational failure. Time and energy must be allocated for outreach to likely learners, many of whom will not appear at the door on their own. Recruitment activities must help potential enrollees realize not only that a service is available, but that it might be an alternative approach to adult education programs with which they might have been uncomfortable or dissatisfied in the past.

One way to identify and recruit adult learners is through community service agencies. Media coverage in the past few years has raised community awareness about the need for literacy and lifelong learning; consequently, building a network of referral sources and gaining access to recruitment sites is relatively easy. Nonetheless, referral agents must be identified and contacted regularly, and the program must be given continuous visibility in appropriate sites.

While adults from all population groups should be encouraged to continue their schooling, the greatest need exists among minorities and immigrant groups. Concerted efforts must be made to gain entry to facilities where people who would benefit most congregate. By brainstorming about connections in the local area, staff persons will come up with many possibilities: foreign language groups, ministers, church workers, social workers, parole officers, senior centers, alcohol treatment centers, drug rehabilitation facilities, army and navy recruitment centers, employment services, job training programs, personnel departments, quality of work life groups, employee education committees, Headstart programs, and facilities for unwed mothers. Once the list is started, it is like unrolling a ball of cord—one name or location leads to another and soon a long line of people and places emerges as the core of a potential recruiting network.

Recruitment is much easier if a personal contact has been established in order to build credibility and gain entry to an organization. An initial meeting might be arranged simply to inform the contact person about the program. Colorful posters and brochures of professional quality, in other languages where appropriate, should be taken to this meeting and left for subsequent use by the contact person as well as for display at the site. One desired outcome of the meeting is that the contact person will have the knowledge and interest to recruit for the program. An even more important outcome is that the person will help arrange meetings with potential enrollees. Meeting with possible enrollees in small groups provides an ideal opportunity to answer questions, respond to apprehensions, and find out best times and locations for classes.

Maintaining communication with the original contact people is essential. Letters of thanks should be written soon after the initial visits. Phone calls or notes can inform them about enrollees from their organizations. New posters and brochures might be taken to the site every two or three months; at the same time, meetings with other groups of potential students can be arranged.

In addition to staff members, adults who are taking classes in the program are often excellent recruiters. They relate well to others in similar circumstances and can share their initial sense of apprehension and subsequent feelings of success. Their recruitment activities might be as simple as talking informally to co-workers and friends. They might team up with other people in a buddy system to lend support in enrolling and attending classes. Some might be willing to participate in organized recruitment activities, perhaps going along to talk about their experiences at some of the group informational meetings in the local agencies. Others might be willing to write testimonials or articles to appear in in-house newsletters, local newspapers, publicity posters, and brochures. Still others might agree to having their photographs displayed on a bulletin board, along with statements about their successes. Videotapes might be made showing interviews of successful participants and shots of their class activities in the local setting. These videotapes could be shown in the cafeteria or lounge at local plants, in the lobby of the social service agencies, and at group recruitment meetings.

Some people will take the first step toward enrolling if, beyond knowing that peers are involved in an adult education program, they feel that the teachers are not strangers to them. To gain visibility, teachers can wear special T-shirts or badges with a logo that identifies the local program. An occasional coffee or lemonade day might be planned during which the teachers serve refreshments and chat informally with people on the plant floor during shift changes or at a table in a local social service agency during peak times. A "get-acquainted" booth might be set up in the cafeteria or at a company picnic or party. Teachers might take walks around the plant, neighborhood, and community centers to make themselves known, as well as to find out about the area. A reception honoring participants and teachers but open to the whole community might encourage some potential enrollees to meet the staff, talk with adults in the program, and get a look at the facilities.

Special services can be provided to create awareness of the program. A book exchange, with a sponsorship sign and a special spot for descriptive brochures about the program, might be set up on a shelf in the reception area, cafeteria, lounge, or near the time clock or payroll office. Current consumer information brochures and other public service announcements might be included for "help yourself" distribution at the same sites. Book raffles, with prizes donated by local bookstores, might be held; free tickets could be distributed and required to be taken to the program location to check for winning numbers and claim prizes.

Special short informational programs (one- or two-hour morning coffees, afternoon teas, or evening events) can be arranged on subjects that would appeal to the general public and to which potential enrollees might bring their families. Topics might include: living with teenagers, helping with homework, improving your memory, or making decisions about whether to buy a computer. A librarian might demonstrate storytelling and reading to children, followed by a related discussion period with parents while the youngsters are taken into another area for a play period. A "computer night" can be arranged at which parents bring their children and the whole family engages in some hands-on experiences at the keyboard. Local people might present an evening of readings of their own prose and poetry. Field trips might be arranged to a local museum, botanical garden, or observatory. A tour might be planned to see how technology is being used in the plant. Whether or not such events attract new enrollees, the programs are worthwhile in themselves, and the very fact that they are offered might sooner or later encourage people who are the target of the outreach to take advantage of opportunities for growth. The involvement of family members in activities has value in providing support and encouragement for educational efforts. As a matter of fact, some workplace adult literacy programs are open to spouses of employees, and perhaps other family members, including children and grandparents, will be added as society moves toward intergenerational learning opportunities.

Easy-to-read printed materials with information about the program should be available. Whenever a recruitment activity is planned, clear, attractive flyers and forms with precise instructions for enrolling in the program should be placed on a table or rack near the door or the refreshments. Attractive bookmarks might be included in paycheck envelopes and inserted in each of the books in the book exchange area mentioned earlier. Posters can be placed on bulletin boards near vending and copy machines in the workplace or in the windows of local stores, gas stations, bars, and social service agencies.

Inquiries and applications should be followed up promptly, whether or not instruction can start right away. For many people, signing up for a program is a major undertaking which should be acknowledged immediately, especially for programs that do not follow the regular schedules of community education night classes whose beginning date and time are fixed. Through a post card, phone call, or personal interview, the learner should be contacted to be assured that the application has been received and to be given information about the time and place for beginning classes. If the starting time is several weeks away, a post card reminder can be sent about a week before the first session.

Recruitment, though not necessarily hard work, is time-consuming but worth the effort. Adults who are convinced of the need to continue their learning may need just the little extra push that the recruitment activities give. Adults who are in most need will be exposed regularly to information about the opportunities. The continuity, persistence, and sincerity of a well-planned campaign might eventually lead to their decision to enroll, whereas without such a campaign they might never respond.

AWARDS AND RECOGNITION CEREMONIES

Learning is its own reward. The excitement of learning gives un-equaled feelings of satisfaction and accomplishment. Awards and recognition ceremonies are manifest capstones that provide oppor-tunities to celebrate those feelings publicly. Awards ceremonies serve two major purposes: (1) recognition from management, union, teachers, and peers on the successful completion of aca-demic tasks, and (2) positive visibility for the program and for the concept of lifelong learning.

The celebration might be held in the plant cafeteria, union hall, or public auditorium, preferably in an area where a reception can be held after the more formal event. A time and day should be chosen during which the learners receiving recognition are most likely to be able to attend. If the program is held in the workplace, released time might be given at least for the participants and their supervisors, if not for all employees. Guests might include family members and friends, co-workers, supervisors, board members, management personnel, union leaders, the mayor, and other com-munity leaders—anyone who has a connection with or an interest in lifelong learning.

The formal event might consist of a few brief remarks from sponsors and teachers, with the major part of the ceremony de-voted to comments from participants in the program and presen-tations of certificates and awards. Certificates might be similar to that shown in Figure 7.1, with no limit to the number that one per-son might acquire, as long as the criteria have been met. Awards should be appropriate to the learners and to the program: books selected specifically for particular individuals, dictionaries, the-sauruses, pens, pencils, and pads of paper containing the motto and logo of the center. Photos of class members and teachers might be taken for distribution to each participant as well as for publicity purposes.

A reception for learners and teachers can follow the awards. The food and drink need not be elaborate, but it should be taste-fully arranged on a linen tablecloth with doilies lining the plates. If possible, coffee and tea servers and punch bowls (not urns and thermos jugs) should be used to fill china (not styrofoam) cups and glasses. Flowers and candles add grace and elegance to the festiv-ity, making a bold statement that the learners and their accom-plishments are important.

```
┌─────────────────────────────────────────────────────────────┐
│  ┌───────────────────────────────────────────────────────┐  │
│  │                                                         │  │
│  │        CERTIFICATE OF ACHIEVEMENT                       │  │
│  │        In Recognition of Participation in               │  │
│  │                                                         │  │
│  │        _____              │  │
│  │                                                         │  │
│  │   This certificate is awarded to_____ │  │
│  │                                                         │  │
│  │   This _____ day of _____ │  │
│  │                                                         │  │
│  │   _____                       │  │
│  │       Director, Lifelong Learning Center                │  │
│  │                                                         │  │
│  │   _____                       │  │
│  │       Instructor, Lifelong Learning Center              │  │
│  │                                                         │  │
│  └───────────────────────────────────────────────────────┘  │
└─────────────────────────────────────────────────────────────┘
```

FIGURE 7.1 Certificate Created on a Macintosh Computer and Printed on a Laser Printer

ASSESSING LEARNER GROWTH

Evaluation is an ongoing process of determining progress. Both teacher and learners in an adult literacy program are continuously involved in assessing growth. In order to determine progress, the evaluators must know where they are heading. There must be a correlation among the program goals, the instructional focus, and the assessment procedures. The first step, then, is to identify the purposes. The major goals of a literacy program are for adults to

1. effectively listen, speak, read, write, participate in groups, and use technology
2. apply those abilities confidently to daily work, home, and social situations
3. feel good about themselves as lifelong learners and participants in all aspects of society

To be valid, assessment must focus on the extent to which the learners exhibit behaviors that indicate accomplishment of those goals. Since the goals relate to purposeful applications and positive attitudes, assessment must be multidimensional to give an overall picture of the learners' achievements. Test results that give grade level scores or indicate that learners can identify specific skills on paper-and-pencil tasks yield very limited information. Despite the fact that our society in general seems quite impressed with measurable results that can be reported numerically, such data fail to match the overall goals. The assumption that numerical scores give evidence of confidence and competence is highly questionable.

How can more comprehensive assessment be realized? Since literacy programs emphasize reading competence to a great extent, suggestions for getting a complete picture of the learner as a reader are given attention here. Both formal and informal assessment procedures should be used to get insights into learners' techniques of interacting with text to construct and reconstruct meanings. Assessment should also indicate the ways in which readers apply the meanings as they gain ever-expanding views of their world. In the next section, some published formal measurement tools are mentioned, with references cited for obtaining more specific information about their use. In the subsequent section, attention is given to a variety of informal assessment techniques to be used by both teachers and learners.

Formal Measures

Formal measures are commercially prepared pre- and post-tests. The results from such tests can serve as guideposts for ongoing informal evaluations by the teacher and learners. The problem, however, is to locate tests that provide information consistent with the goals of the program. Few published tests for adults are available, and the ones that are on the market focus primarily on knowledge about discrete word recognition and comprehension skills. If assessment is to be helpful, attention needs to be on the reader's *use* of strategies, not simply the ability to recognize words, identify letter–sound relationships, or pick a multiple-choice answer for a comprehension question.

A few tools that might yield some insights about applications of skills are: (1) Woodcock Passage Comprehension Subtest (Woodcock, 1987) to provide information on the learner's ability to use semantic and syntactic cueing systems while reading, (2) Wood-cock Word Identification Subtest (Woodcock, 1987) to judge the learner's ability to apply basic phonic and syllabication rules, and (3) Bader Visual Discrimination Test (Bader, 1983) to indicate particular letters and mode of presentation for which a problem might exist.

The Reading Miscue Inventory (Goodman & Burke, 1972) is a valuable tool. Although it is not a test in the conventional sense, it is a formal procedure when used in its entirety. Teachers who are familiar with the principles on which it is based will have valuable insights into reading behaviors in lessons, even though they do not use it as a formal assessment procedure. The Miscue Inventory provides information on the learner's ability to use grapho-phonemic, syntactic, and semantic cueing systems while in the process of reading complete passages. The term "miscue" is used to indicate that deviations between printed text and oral reading are considered clues to the reader's processes, rather than deemed wrong or undesirable. Miscues include substitutions, additions, omissions, mispronunciations, and self-corrections.

In the formal use of the inventory, the oral reading is taped so that the miscues can be analyzed later. Each miscue is analyzed qualitatively as to the extent to which it maintains the sense of the passage (semantically acceptable), sounds like language (syntactically acceptable), and looks and sounds like the printed word (grapho-phonemically similar). A judgment is made as to whether substitutions or pronunciation differences are acceptable in the reader's dialect. Successful self-corrections are important indications that the reader is comprehending.

In addition to the clues to meaning revealed during oral reading, comprehension is assessed by having the reader retell the passage. The retelling can be prompted by a general question such as, "What was this passage about?" Following the free response to the general question, the reader can be asked follow-up questions that build upon the information offered during the retelling. For example, the reader might be asked, "What more can you tell about . . . (character, event, problem, or event mentioned in the retelling)?"

Teachers who are familiar with miscue analysis are alert to the quality of, and possible reasons for, miscues during oral reading. They allow and encourage readers to read on and, if necessary, correct themselves, rather than stop to figure out words the minute they digress from the printed text. For a comprehensive explanation of adapting the principles of miscue analysis to ongoing evaluation and instruction, see Goodman, Watson, and Burke (1987).

Informal Techniques

A portfolio of a learner's work, which includes writings as well as records of various types of periodic assessments, is a rich and meaningful source of information about progress. The grid in Figure 7.2 gives an overview of informal evaluation tools; what they assess; how and when they might be administered; the type of scoring, if any; and how results are determined. A battery of tools can be used, including forms for recording books read and keeping track of spelling and vocabulary growth, files and recordings of writings and oral readings, anecdotal records by both teacher and learners, reading behavior questionnaires, writing assessments (included because of the strong connections between reading and writing), and attendance records. All of these tools are used in ways that present a positive focus on strengths, progress, and applications, not on weaknesses, deficiencies, and isolated skills.

Individual Records and Graphs.   The first two items on the grid refer to regular record-keeping procedures that are integral parts of lessons. The use of file folders to maintain a portfolio of individual records and graphs is described in Chapter 2. The "Books Read" form is simply a page on which the learner records book titles and completion dates for every book read (see Figure 2.2). Many learners had previously never completed a book, and they are rewarded to see lengthening lists of books they have read. The titles reflect broadening and deepening reading interests. The insights gained about these interests are useful for teachers in planning lessons that relate to learners' concerns.

Spelling progress and vocabulary development are recorded on graphs (see Figure 2.3). As mentioned in Chapter 2, learners might keep boxes of vocabulary cards with words chosen from their writings. They can be asked to recognize, use in context, and spell a random sample of ten to twelve words from those cards every two weeks. On subsequent tests, students have another chance with words missed. Learners are responsible for graphing their successes in the biweekly tests.

Anecdotal Records.   Anecdotes, retellings of situations that illustrate a success or positive change for an individual, may be

(*text continues on p. 176*)

FIGURE 7.2 Assessment Grid

ASSESSMENT TOOL	COGNITIVE PROCESSES & AFFECTIVE FACTORS	HOW ADMINISTERED	TYPE OF SCORING	HOW RESULTS ARE DETERMINED	WHEN ADMINISTERED
Books Read Form	reading interests; reading volume	self-report		count of number and types read	continuous
Spelling and Vocabulary Graph	spelling; word meaning; word recognition	individually by instructor	graph	number correct out of 10	every 2 weeks
Anecdotal Records (Teacher)	reading process; writing process; attitude	teacher-generated observation or learner report	assessment by teacher	teacher's perception of change	one every 10 weeks
Anecdotal Records (Learner)	reading process; writing process; attitude	learner-generated	self-evaluation	learner's perception of change	one every 10 weeks

Writing Assessment	writing process	unaided writing in response to stimulus article read by group	holistic ratings by trained raters in 3 areas: authenticity, focus, and language	comparison of pre- and post-scores in 3 areas: authenticity, focus, and language	entry; every 20 weeks
Reading Behavior Questionnaire	reading interest; reading attitude; reading strategies	self-report	rating scale	comparison of pre- and post-ratings	entry; after 10 weeks; after 20 weeks
Attendance	attitude; appropriateness of instruction	learner-kept attendance record; instructor record		numerical count	

written by learners and teachers. Learners record their perceptions of changes that have occurred in their lives. The changes might relate to things that they feel more confident doing, such as balancing a checkbook or ordering lumber, or applications of newly learned procedures, such as measuring for wallpaper. Teachers' anecdotes are based on their perceptions of changes taking place and incidents told to them by learners. It is important that teachers point out changes because learners are often too involved in the process to see that growth has indeed occurred.

Lucy's successes can be seen from this incident described by her teacher.

> *April 15.* Lucy G. is becoming acquainted with the public libraries in the area. She now has cards for [two local libraries]. Last Sunday, Lucy's sister tried repeatedly to call her but to no avail. She was amazed and excited that evening when Lucy told her that she and Susie, her eight-year-old daughter, had spent the entire afternoon at the . . . Branch Library. They had both checked out books, two for Lucy and three for Susie. In the past, Lucy's sister had tried unsuccessfully to get her interested in books and involved in reading. Lucy told her sister about the reading and writing class she is taking and explained how it has stimulated her interest in books.

The following anecdote, written by Allen's teacher, indicates that he can not only apply techniques but can convince other teachers of their merit:

> *Nov. 7.* A teacher from the educational program in the . . . plant visited our program. She was very impressed with what she saw. While observing, she met Allen P., who was writing a story by using the clustering technique. He explained how he and his teacher had brainstormed on paper; this gave him vocabulary and ideas to guide him when writing. Our visitor noted the effectiveness of this method. Allen gave the teacher a copy of a story he had written previously about his job as a utility and relief man on the shock line. The teacher felt Allen's story might inspire some of her learners to write about their jobs. Allen felt pleased that his story will be used to help other writers.

Such anecdotes corroborate the learner's progress and also indicate affective changes that are often noted but not documented. A schedule might be set up so that these important records are not neglected. The teacher, for example, might plan to write at least one anecdote about each learner during every eight- to ten-week class.

Learners might be asked to keep sections in their journals (described in Chapter 2) where they respond periodically to a question such as: What has changed for me personally, socially, behaviorally, culturally, or intellectually? Note Paul's delight in his newfound ability.

> I wrote a letter to my son about two weeks ago. I feel great about it. This class gave me the confidence to do it. This is the first time I wrote to my son. He wrote me a letter back instead of a phone call like he usually does. I was really surprised. Thank you for helping me.

Linda indicates that she uses mapping, a reading technique to show the organization of a story or chapter, with her five-year-old son.

> *March 10.* I love mapping. It helps me remember what I read. Last Sunday Dustin and I mapped "The Gingerbread Man."

Writing Assessment.   Files of dated original writings accomplished during classes (as described in Chapter 2) provide visible means of viewing progress. A copy of the first writing should be kept in the learner's portfolio. If early writing is cooperatively done (dictated to the teacher), then copies of both the first dictated piece and the first independent writing should be kept. Writing growth can be assessed informally by having learners select three writings from their portfolios, representing their work over a period of time. By placing these writings in time sequence, learners can readily see the changes they have made. Their self-evaluative comments can be recorded by the teacher and added to the anecdotal records.

These informal determinations of growth from writing samples can be supplemented by more formal writing assessment procedures. For the formal periodic writing assessments, learners write unaided in response to a stimulus article. An initial writing completed upon entry to the program provides a baseline for ongoing assessments. Subsequent writings to assess growth can be elicited every 10 weeks, or at intervals deemed appropriate for particular learners and situations. Trained raters use qualitative criteria, examples of which are given below, to judge the content and quality of the writing.

The initial, or pre-writing, assessment might be carried out during the second class meeting. By delaying until the second session, the teacher can establish some rapport with the learners to alleviate some of the anxieties about writing. The assessment is conducted just as in the writing phase of a regular class (as described in Chapter 2). Learners first read a stimulus article or study a picture or cartoon. In the ensuing discussion, the teacher encourages the learners to share reactions and to question themselves and others in the group. They are prompted to think in terms of the question "Why do you think . . . ?" The clustering technique can be incorporated within the lesson. Learners are then given 30 minutes to write their thoughts. After the writing, the papers are collected and the names of writers are replaced with numbers to ensure anonymity when the papers are rated.

Guidelines such as the following, adapted from *The High School Writing Project* (Ann Arbor High School Teachers, 1984), might be used for rating the papers. The criteria refer to three aspects that indicate the writer's involvement and interaction with materials: authenticity, focus, and language. Each of these aspects is rated on a four-point scale.

A. Authenticity/voice/engagement of the reader
   4 = Expression strongly reflects the writer's emotional and/ or intellectual involvement in the topic. Strongly engages the attention of the reader.
   3 = The writer is engaged in the topic and engages the reader.
   2 = Uninteresting; not engaging; perfunctory.
   1 = Writing seems to be a mechanical exercise. Marked by clichés, hazy generalization, meaningless expressions.
B. Focus/organization/development
   4 = Focuses on one main idea. Has clear beginning, middle, and end. Well-organized and well-developed through examples.
   3 = Focused and organized but may have a flaw in coherence or incomplete closure. Incomplete development. Explanation is strongly implicit.
   2 = Lack of clear focus, organization, or development. Narrative but not explanation.
   1 = Disorganized; undeveloped; unconnected generalizations.
C. Sentence mechanics/language
   4 = Few mechanical, usage, or sentence errors. Language used with fluency and variety.
   3 = Some minor mechanical usage or sentence errors. Language used competently to express ideas.

2 = Enough usage errors to attract attention away from the
content. Sentences understandable, but unconventional.
1 = Language and mechanical errors impair meaning.

If possible, two raters should judge the writings. The raters should have some preliminary practice on several written selections to gain familiarity with the rating scale. First the sample selections should be judged individually by the raters. Then they can meet to discuss the reasons for their assignment of specific values to each writing. Once the procedure is understood, papers can be scored by two raters and their ratings averaged for each of the three items. While such an activity might seem time-consuming, it is one way to assign a quantitative score to an assessment centered on the quality of content and the involvement of the learner in thinking and writing processes. Furthermore, teachers who become involved in evaluating writing in this manner will undoubtedly carry over the principles to class settings as they conduct and evaluate writing activities.

Reading Behavior Questionnaire. A Reading Behavior Questionnaire (see Appendix B) is an instrument that provides information concerning learners' reading interests and habits and their knowledge and use of reading strategies. In Part A of that instrument, the learner indicates his or her self-perceptions as a reader and the extent to which he or she reads and writes various types of materials. Parts B through E elicit information about metacognitive dimensions, that is, the learner's awareness and use of comprehension strategies. Specifically, the questionnaire asks the learner to indicate the use of particular strategies before, during, and after reading as well as the application of study skills. The teacher reads items on the reading behavior questionnaire aloud, thus facilitating administration of the instrument with learners at various reading levels.

When such a questionnaire is administered at the beginning of a class, the teacher gets insights into learners' feelings, interests, and reading behaviors that can be used as an aid in planning appropriate instruction. Administering the questionnaire again at the end of an eight- or ten-week session makes it possible to determine changes in perceptions and strategic behaviors. Although this self-report format is subject to all of the problems of learner-reported instruments, it does provide information that is difficult, if not impossible, to obtain in any other way. The results are probably more valid for adults than for children and adolescents.

Attendance.   Finally, of course, attendance is a means of assessment. Although attending class does not necessarily mean that progress is being made, it does give an indication of the learner's attitudes and may reflect whether the instruction is appropriate. Attendance is particularly significant with working adults because they have limited time for attending classes and will not continue if they do not feel they are being successful.

Records kept by individual learners provide an incentive for them to maintain regular attendance and assume responsibility for learning (see Figure 2.1). A minimum number of class sessions attended and writings completed might be used as criteria for the awards given at the semiannual ceremonies described earlier in this chapter.

SUMMARY: LEARNING IS FOREVER

Learning continues long after schooling is completed. Viable programs to invite adult learners and maintain their involvement must be carefully planned, continually evaluated, modified to meet changing demands, and publicized. Opportunities for life-long learning are essential for individual and societal benefits. This means that funding agencies must be presented with proposals for well-planned educational programs that convince them to provide moral support, financial assistance, and physical facilities for adult learning centers in the community and the workplace. Recruitment efforts must be designed so that all potential learners, including those who are hardest to reach, know that educational opportunities exist and that content, procedures, and facilities have been developed specifically for adults. Evidence of progress toward functional literacy should be gathered through evaluation techniques that indicate growth related to the major goals of learning to learn and feeling good about one's accomplishments. The efforts of adult learners should be respected and their accomplishments recognized and celebrated.

Meaningful education enriches people and affects them for a lifetime. Involvement in dynamic, interactive programs engages adults in purposeful learning that gives more dimension to their work and personal lives. The benefits spread to family, friends, and the community as a whole. The short phrase "lifelong learning" is long in impact—learning is forever!

APPENDIXES

REFERENCES

INDEX

ABOUT THE AUTHORS

Appendix A
Computer Questionnaire

Name _____ Date _____

Place of birth (state/country) _____

Please help us by providing the following information. Your answers will be kept confidential. If there is any personal information you prefer not to give, leave that item blank.

A. Please answer the following questions about your background.

    1. Employment status

        _____ employed
        _____ retired
        _____ laid-off
        _____ unemployed
        _____ other: _____

    2. Age

        _____ 16–20
        _____ 21–30
        _____ 31–40
        _____ 41–50
        _____ 51–60
        _____ 61–70
        _____ 71–80

    3. Sex   _____female   _____male

    4. Marital status

        _____ single
        _____ married
        _____ divorced
        _____ widow/er

    5. Number of dependent children_____

6. Highest level of schooling

_____ 0–6 years

_____ 7–9 years

_____ 10–12 years

_____ high school diploma

_____ GED certificate

_____ 1–2 years college

_____ 3–4 years college

_____ more than 4 years college

B. Computer Background

1. Why are you taking this course? Check only one answer.

_____ curiosity

_____ to improve my job skills

_____ to purchase a computer

_____ pressure from boss

_____ to keep up with my children

_____ to learn to use my computer

_____ other (please explain) _____

2. How many computer classes have you taken?

_____ 0 (none)

_____ 1

_____ 2

_____ 3

_____ more than 3

3. If you have taken a computer course, where did you take it?

_____ computer store

_____ university

_____ community college

_____ adult education

_____ other: _____

4. Is there a microcomputer in your home?_____ yes _____no

5. If yes, do you use it?_____ yes_____ no

6. Is there a microcomputer at your work station?
_____yes _____no

7. If yes, do you use it?_____ yes _____no

8. Is there computerized equipment (other than a microcomputer) at your work station? _____yes_____ no

9. Please write the number that best describes how much you have used the following:

   1 = not at all
   2 = used some
   3 = used a lot
   _____ video games (in an arcade; e.g., *Pac-Man*)
   _____ games on a microcomputer
   _____ word processing
   _____ database
   _____ spreadsheet
   _____ graphics
   _____ Logo
   _____ BASIC

10. How well do you type?
    _____ very well
    _____ a little bit
    _____ none

11. If you type, how do you type?
    _____ hunt and peck
    _____ touch-type

12. If you do not type well, are you worried that your lack of typing skills will interfere with your use of computers?
    _____yes _____no

13. Please write a number that indicates your understanding of each of the terms below:

    1 = Never heard of this term
    2 = Heard the term but not sure what it means
    3 = Could give a general description of it
    4 = Could give a detailed description of it

    _____ DOS
    _____ boot
    _____ disk
    _____ disk drive
    _____ RAM
    _____ ROM
    _____ files
    _____ Logo
    _____ BASIC

14. Please write the number that best fits your understanding of the *uses* of each of the following:

    1 = Never heard of it
    2 = Heard of it but not sure what it's used for
    3 = Could describe the general uses of it
    4 = Could give a detailed description of its uses

    _____ word processing
    _____ database
    _____ spelling checker
    _____ graphs
    _____ spreadsheet
    _____ integrated package

15. Please write a number indicating your *opinion* about each statement below. There are no wrong answers.

    1 = strongly agree
    2 = agree
    3 = disagree
    4 = strongly disagree

    _____ Computers are smarter than people.
    _____ I would feel comfortable using a computer.
    _____ Computers make everyday life easier.
    _____ Computers do only what they are told.
    _____ I need to know a programming language (like BASIC) to use a computer.
    _____ Computers are always right.
    _____ The idea of using a computer scares me.
    _____ I need to know a lot about math to use computers.
    _____ I would like to have a computer at home.
    _____ Computers will put people out of work.
    _____ Computers think like people.
    _____ Using a computer would make my job easier.

16. Please write a number indicating how *confident* you feel about using the items listed below:

    1 = I can't use this at all.
    2 = I think I can use this but I might need some help.
    3 = I can use this confidently on my own.

    _____ a menu on a commercial program
    _____ printer
    _____ function keys
    _____ disk drive
    _____ DOS

Appendix B
Reading Behavior Questionnaire

READING BEHAVIOR QUESTIONNAIRE

Name: _____ Date: _____ PRE   POST

This is a questionnaire to find out about your reading. THERE ARE NO RIGHT OR WRONG ANSWERS. The instructor will read each question out loud. Answer each question by circling the response closest to what is true for you. If you have questions, feel free to ask. Please be honest about your behavior.

A. READING BACKGROUND

1. How often do you read?

Very Often	Often	Sometimes	Seldom	Never
5	4	3	2	1

If you never read, please stop here.

2. If you do read, what do you like to read? (Circle as many as you like.)

Newspapers	Novels	Bible
History	Magazines	Short stories
Manuals/reports	Romance	How-to books
Comics	Mystery	Poetry

Other: _____
(please describe)

3. How good are you at reading each of the following? (Circle one answer for each type of reading.)

	Poor		Average		Excellent
Newspapers	1	2	3	4	5
Novels	1	2	3	4	5
Technical material	1	2	3	4	5
Magazines	1	2	3	4	5
Signs	1	2	3	4	5

4. How often do you have to do work-related reading?

Very Often	Often	Sometimes	Seldom	Never
5	4	3	2	1

5. If you do work-related reading, what do you read? (Circle as many as you like.)

Charts   Graphs

Blueprints   Operating instructions

Trouble-shooting charts   Repair manuals

Assembly procedures

6. How often do you read to children?

Very Often	Often	Sometimes	Seldom	Never
5	4	3	2	1

7. How often do you write?

Very Often	Often	Sometimes	Seldom	Never
5	4	3	2	1

8. If you do write, what do you write? (Circle as many as you like.)

Notes	Letters	Lists
Forms	Reports	Diary/journal
Fiction	Poetry	Non-fiction
Prayers		

B. BEFORE READING

Before you _start_ to read a story or article:

		Very Often	Often	Sometimes	Seldom	Never
9.	How often do you think about why you're going to read the story or article?	5	4	3	2	1
10.	How often do you read titles?	5	4	3	2	1
11.	How often do you read the captions of pictures, maps, or graphs that go with a story or article?	5	4	3	2	1
12.	How often do you look over the story or article from beginning to end?	5	4	3	2	1
13.	How often do you predict what the story or article is about?	5	4	3	2	1
14.	How often do you think about what you _already_ know about a topic?	5	4	3	2	1
15.	How often do you think about what you want to learn from the reading?	5	4	3	2	1

C. DURING READING

When you come to a word you don't know while reading:

		Very Often	Often	Sometimes	Seldom	Never
16.	How often do you skip the word or words?	5	4	3	2	1
17.	How often do you break the word into syllables?	5	4	3	2	1
18.	How often do you break the word into meaningful parts? (example: trans-form)	5	4	3	2	1
19.	How often do you sound the word out?	5	4	3	2	1
20.	How often do you use the other words in the sentence or paragraph to try to figure it out?	5	4	3	2	1

C. DURING READING (continued)

When you come to a word you don't know while reading:

		Very Often	Often	Sometimes	Seldom	Never
21.	How often do you use the dictionary?	5	4	3	2	1
22.	How often do you ask someone else?	5	4	3	2	1

When you read:

		Very Often	Often	Sometimes	Seldom	Never
23.	How often do you find sentences hard to understand?	5	4	3	2	1
24.	How often do you find paragraphs hard to understand?	5	4	3	2	1

To understand what you read:

		Very Often	Often	Sometimes	Seldom	Never
25.	How often do you reread parts of the article or story?	5	4	3	2	1
26.	How often do you skip the sentence or paragraph?	5	4	3	2	1
27.	How often do you make predictions or guesses about the reading?	5	4	3	2	1
28.	How often do you see pictures in your mind when you read?	5	4	3	2	1
29.	How often do you ask yourself questions while reading?	5	4	3	2	1
30.	How often do you think about what the story or article means while you're reading?	5	4	3	2	1
31.	How often do you try to relate the reading to things you already know?	5	4	3	2	1
32.	How often do you try to relate the reading to situations in your own life?	5	4	3	2	1

C. DURING READING (continued)

To understand what you read:

	Very Often	Often	Sometimes	Seldom	Never
33. How often do you pick out key words?	5	4	3	2	1
34. How often do you summarize the reading in your own words?	5	4	3	2	1
35. How often do you ask someone else what the article or story means?	5	4	3	2	1

D. AFTER READING

When you have finished reading:

	Very Often	Often	Sometimes	Seldom	Never
36. How often do you think about what the story or article was about?	5	4	3	2	1
37. How often do you think about why you read the story or article?	5	4	3	2	1
38. How often do you think about related experiences in your own life?	5	4	3	2	1
39. How often do you compare what you've read to other reading materials?	5	4	3	2	1
40. How often do you think about sharing ideas with someone else?	5	4	3	2	1
41. How often do you discuss the content with others?	5	4	3	2	1
42. How often do you think about getting additional information on the topic of the reading?	5	4	3	2	1

E. STUDY SKILLS

When you are reading a textbook or training materials:

	Very Often	Often	Sometimes	Seldom	Never
43. How often do you look over the material before you start to read?	5	4	3	2	1
44. How often do you skim the chapter?	5	4	3	2	1
45. How often do you read the questions at the end of the story or article?	5	4	3	2	1
46. How often do you see pictures in your mind when you read?	5	4	3	2	1
47. How often do you ask yourself questions while you read?	5	4	3	2	1
48. How often do you make predictions or guesses as you read?	5	4	3	2	1
49. How often do you change your speed as you read?	5	4	3	2	1
50. How often do you reread?	5	4	3	2	1
51. How often do you underline or highlight parts?	5	4	3	2	1
52. How often do you take notes?	5	4	3	2	1
53. How often do you summarize in your own words?	5	4	3	2	1
54. How often do you compare what you've read to other readings?	5	4	3	2	1
55. How often do you review what you've read?	5	4	3	2	1
56. How often do you discuss the reading with someone else?	5	4	3	2	1
57. How often do you try to memorize?	5	4	3	2	1

Thank You For Answering These Questions!
Please Give This Form To Your Instructor.

Appendix C
Organizations and Journals About Adult Literacy

Many national organizations provide support, information, and opportunities for networking with people involved in adult literacy initiatives. A representative list of some of the organizations available to teachers and administrators follows. Many of the organizations publish journals or newsletters. The names of journals that have been particularly helpful to the authors are included with the address of the organization. The authors make no claim that this is a comprehensive list and would be pleased to have information about other organizations and publications related to adult literacy.

Adult Literacy and Technology Project
PCC, Inc.
2682 Bishop Drive, Suite 107
San Ramon, CA 94503

American Association for Adult and Continuing Education (AAACE)
1201 16th Street, N.W.
Suite 230
Washington, DC 20036
Journal: *Adult Learning* (formerly *Lifelong Learning*)

American Library Association
50 E. Huron Street
Chicago, IL 60611

American Newspaper Publishers Association (ANPA)
Manager of Literacy Programs
P. O. Box 17407
Dulles International Airport
Washington, DC 20041

American Society for Training and Development (ASTD)
1630 Duke Street
Box 1443
Alexandria, VA 22313
Journal: *Training and Development Journal*

American Vocational Association
1410 King Street
Alexandria, VA 22314

Association for Community-Based Education (ACBE)
1806 Vernon Street, N.W.
Washington, DC 20009

The Barbara Bush Foundation for Family Literacy
1002 Wisconsin Avenue, N.W.
Washington, DC 20007

Business Council for Effective Literacy (BCEL)
1221 Avenue of the Americas, 35th Floor
New York, NY 10020

Coalition for Literacy
50 E. Huron Street
Chicago, IL 60611

Commission on Adult Basic Education
1201 16th Street, N.W., Suite 230
Washington, DC 20036

Correctional Education Association
4321 Hartwick Road, Suite L–208
College Park, MD 20740

Institute for the Study of Adult Illiteracy
Pennsylvania State University
248 Calder Way, Room 307
University Park, PA 16801

International Reading Association (IRA)
800 Barksdale Road
P. O. Box 8139
Newark, DE 19714–8139
Journal: *Journal of Reading*

Laubach Literacy International
1320 Jamesville Avenue
P. O. Box 131
Syracuse, NY 13210

Literacy Volunteers of America, Inc. (LVA)
5795 Widewaters Parkway
Syracuse, NY 13214

National Advisory Council of Adult Education (NACAE)
2000 L. Street, N.W., Suite 570
Washington, DC 20036

National Community Education Association
119 N. Payne Street
Alexandria, VA 22314

National Council of State Directors of Adult Education
Division of Adult Education
New York State Department of Education
Washington Avenue
Albany, NY 12234

National Council of Teachers of English
1111 Kenyon Road
Urbana, IL 61801
Journal: *The English Journal*

Project Literacy U.S. (PLUS)
Box 2, 4802 Fifth Avenue
Pittsburgh, PA 15213

U.S. Department of Education
Adult Literacy Initiative (ALI)
Reporter's Building, Room 510
400 Maryland Avenue, S.W.
Washington, DC 20202

U.S. Department of Education
Division of Adult Education
400 Maryland Avenue, S.W.
Washington, DC 20202

U.S. Department of Labor
Employment and Training Administration
200 Constitution Avenue, N.W.
Washington, DC 20210

References

PROFESSIONAL REFERENCES

Anderson, R. C., Hiebert, E. H., Scott, J. A., & Wilkinson, I. A. G. (1985). *Becoming a nation of readers: The report of the Commission on Reading.* Urbana, IL: Center for the Study of Reading.

Ann Arbor High School Teachers. (1984). *Instructions for Administering the Ann Arbor High School Writing Assessment.* Unpublished manuscript.

Applebee, A. N., Langer, J. A., & Mullis, I. V. S. (1987). *Learning to be literate in America: Reading, writing, and reasoning.* Princeton, NJ: Educational Testing Service.

Bader, L. (1983). *Reading and language inventory.* New York: Macmillan.

Bransford, J. D., & Johnson, M. K. (1972). Contextual prerequisites for understanding: Some investigations of comprehension and recall. *Journal of Verbal Learning and Verbal Behavior, 11*, 717–726.

Brookfield, S. D. (1986a). Media power and the development of media literacy: An adult educational interpretation. *Harvard Educational Review, 56*, 151–170.

Brookfield, S. D. (1986b). *Understanding and facilitating adult learning.* San Francisco: Jossey-Bass.

Calkins, L. M. (1986). *The art of teaching writing.* Portsmouth, NH: Heinemann.

Coles, W. E., Jr. (1983, Winter). The literacy crisis: A challenge how? *Fforum Newsletter, 4*, 114–121.

Downing, J. (1982). Reading: Skill or skills? *The Reading Teacher, 35*, 534–537.

Elbow, P. (1973). *Writing without teachers.* New York: Oxford University Press.

Emig, J. (1983). *The web of meaning: Essays on writing, teaching, learning and thinking.* Upper Montclair, NJ: Boynton/Cook.

Farr, R., & Carey, R. F. (1986). *Reading: What can be measured?* Newark, DE: International Reading Association.

Fulwiler, T. (1987). *Teaching with writing.* Portsmouth, NH: Boynton/Cook.

Goldberg, N. (1986). *Writing down the bones.* Boston, MA: Shambhala Publications.

Goodman, K. S. (1986). *What's whole in whole language?* New York: Heine-mann.

Goodman, K. S., Goodman, Y. M., & Hood, W. J. (Eds.). (1989). *The whole language evaluation book.* Portsmouth, NH: Heinemann.

Goodman, K. S., Smith, E. B., Meredith, R., & Goodman, Y. M. (1987). *Language and thinking in school: A whole-language curriculum* (3rd ed.). New York: Richard C. Owen.

Goodman, Y. M., & Burke, C. L. (1972). *Reading miscue inventory: Manual.* New York: Macmillan.

Goodman, Y., Watson, D., & Burke, C. (1987). *Reading miscue inventory: Alternative procedures.* New York: Richard C. Owen.

Graves, D. H. (1984). *A researcher learns to write.* Exeter, NH: Heinemann.

Hansen, J. (1987). *When writers read.* Portsmouth, NH: Heinemann.

Harman, D. (1987). *Illiteracy: A national dilemma.* New York: Cambridge Book Company.

Heimlich, J. E., & Pittelman, S. D. (1986). *Semantic mapping: Classroom applications.* Newark, DE: International Reading Association.

Hunter, C. S. J., & Harman, D. (1979). *Adult literacy in the United States: A report to the Ford Foundation.* New York: McGraw-Hill.

Jensen, J. M. (Ed.). (1984). *Composing and comprehending.* Urbana, IL: ERIC Clearinghouse on Reading and Communication Skills and the National Conference on Research in English.

Johnson, D. W., & Johnson, F. P. (1987). *Joining together: Group therapy and group skills.* Englewood Cliffs, NJ: Prentice-Hall.

Johnston, W. B. (1986). *Workforce 2000: Work and workers for the 21st century.* Washington, DC: U.S. Department of Labor.

Kazemek, F. E., & Rigg, P. (1985a). *Adult illiteracy—America's phoenix problem.* Tucson: University of Arizona.

Kazemek, F. E., & Rigg, P. (1985b). For adults only: Reading materials for adult literacy students. *Journal of Reading, 28,* 726–731.

Kirsch, I. S., & Jungeblut, A. (1986). *Literacy: Profiles of America's young adults.* Princeton, NJ: Educational Testing Service.

Knowles, M. S., & Associates. (1984). *Andragogy in action: Applying modern principles of adult learning.* San Francisco: Jossey-Bass.

McNeil, J. D. (1987). *Reading comprehension: New directions for classroom practice* (2nd ed.). Glenview, IL: Scott, Foresman.

Michigan Reading Association. (1985). *Guidelines for evaluating reading software.* Grand Rapids: Michigan Reading Association.

Murray, D. (1982). *Learning by teaching: Selected articles on writing and teaching.* Montclair, NJ: Boynton/Cook.

Ornstein, A. C. (1987, May). Questioning: The essence of good teaching. *NASSP Bulletin, 71*(499), 71–79.

Pearson, P. D. (Ed.). (1984). *Handbook of reading research.* New York: Long-man.

Pearson, P. D., & Tierney, R. J. (1984). *On becoming a thoughtful reader:*

Learning to read like a writer. (Reading Education Report No. 50). Urbana, IL: Center for the Study of Reading. (ERIC Document Reproduction Service No. ED 247 530)

Postman, N., & Weingartner, C. (1969). *Teaching as a subversive activity.* New York: Delacorte Press.

Rico, G. L. (1983). *Writing the natural way.* Los Angeles: J. P. Tarcher.

Rubin, A., & Hansen, J. (1986). Reading and writing: How are the first two "R's" related? In J. Orasanu (Ed.), *Reading comprehension: From research to practice* (pp. 163–171). Hillsdale, NJ: Lawrence Erlbaum Associates.

Rumelhart, D. (1977). Toward an interactive model of reading. In S. Dornic (Ed.), *Attention and performance* (pp. 573–603). Hillsdale, NJ: Lawrence Erlbaum Associates.

Samuels, S. J. (1976). Hierarchical subskills in the reading acquisition process. In J. T. Guthrie (Ed.), *Aspects of reading acquisition.* Baltimore, MD: Johns Hopkins University Press.

Smith, F. (1973). *Psycholinguistics and reading.* New York: Holt, Rinehart & Winston.

Smith, R. (1986, June). Speech to Michigan Private Industry Council, Lansing, Michigan.

Soifer, R., Young, D., & Irwin, M. E. (1989). The Academy: A learner-centered workplace literacy program. In A. Fingeret & P. Jurmo (Eds.), *Participatory literacy education.* San Francisco: Jossey-Bass.

Sommers, N., & McQuade, D. (1989). *Student writers at work and in the company of other writers: The Bedford prizes.* New York: St. Martin's Press.

U. S. Department of Labor and U. S. Department of Education. (1988). *The bottom line: Basic skills in the workplace.* Washington, DC: Office of Public Information, Employment and Training Administration, U. S. Department of Labor.

Valencia, S., & Pearson, P. D. (1987). Reading assessment: Time for a change. *The Reading Teacher, 40,* 726–732.

Van Nostrand, A. D. (1979). Writing and the generation of knowledge. *Social Education, 43,* 178–180.

White, M. A. (Ed.). (1987). *What curriculum for the information age?* Hillsdale, NJ: Lawrence Erlbaum Associates.

Wisxon, K. K., Peters, C. W., Weber, E. M., & Roeber, E. D. (1987). New directions in statewide reading assessment. *The Reading Teacher, 40,* 749–754.

Woodcock, R. W. (1987). *Woodcock Reading Master Tests-Revised.* Circle Pines, MN: American Guidance Service.

Young, D., & Irwin, M. (1988). Integrating computers into adult literacy programs. *Journal of Reading, 31,* 648–652.

Zinsser, W. (1985). *On writing well.* New York: Harper & Row.

Zinsser, W. (1988). *Writing to learn.* New York: Harper & Row.

MATERIALS FOR ADULT LEARNERS

Print Materials

Blackman, M. C. (1970). A good little feature. In *Against all odds* (pp. 118–121). New York: Noble and Noble.

Burke, N. (1970). Polar night. In *Against all odds* (pp. 59–69). New York: Noble and Noble.

Capote, T. (1980). A Christmas memory. In *Best short stories: Short stories for teaching literature and developing comprehension: Advanced level* (pp. 297–305). Providence, RI: Jamestown Publishers.

Crane, S. (1968). A dark brown dog. In *Uptight, the name of the game* (pp. 55–60). Jericho, NY: New Dimensions in Education.

Digilio, K. S. (1987). *GED social studies.* Chicago: Contemporary Books.

GED Testing Service. (1985). *The 1988 Tests of General Educational Development: A Preview.* Washington, DC: American Council on Education.

Howett, J. (1987). *GED mathematics.* Chicago: Contemporary Books.

Hughes, L. (1967). Mother to son. In *Courage under fire* (p. 24). Columbus, OH: Charles E. Merrill.

Mitchell, R. (1987). *GED science.* Chicago: Contemporary Books.

Momaday, N. S. (1969). *The way to rainy mountain.* Albuquerque: The University of New Mexico Press.

News for you. Published weekly by New Readers Press, Division of Laubach Literacy International, P.O. Box 131, Syracuse, NY 13210.

Romanek, E. (1987). *GED Literature and the Arts.* Chicago: Contemporary Books.

Swenson, M. (1986). Southbound on the freeway. In *The reader's anthology* (p. 114). New York: Globe Book Company.

Wickham, S. B. (1987). *GED writing skills.* Chicago: Contemporary Books.

Software

Birth of the Phoenix. American Eagle Software, Inc., P.O. Box 46080, Lincolnwood, Il 60646.

Comprehension Connection. Milliken Publishing Company, 1100 Research Boulevard, St. Louis, MO 63132.

Crossword Magic. Mindscape, Inc., 3444 Dundee Road, Northbrook, IL 60062.

Decisions, Decisions. Tom Snyder Productions, 90 Sherman Street, Cambridge, MA 02140.

Expedition U.S.A.! Society for Visual Education, Inc., 1345 Diversey Parkway, Chicago, IL 60614–1299.

Geometric Supposer. Sunburst Communications, 39 Washington Avenue, Pleasantville, NY 10570–2898.

Hinky Pinky. Learning Well Publishing Co., 200 S. Service Road, Roslyn Heights, NY 11577.

Interviews with History. Educational Publishing Concepts, Inc., P.O. Box 715, St. Charles, IL 60174.

M-ss-ng L-nks. Sunburst Communications, 39 Washington Avenue, Pleasantville, NY 10570–2898.

The Puzzler. Sunburst Communications, 39 Washington Avenue, Pleasantville, NY 10570–2898.

Reading Realities. Teacher Support Software, P. O. Box 7125, Gainesville, FL 32605–7125.

The Secret of Vincent's Museum. Tom Snyder Productions, 90 Sherman Street, Cambridge, MA 02140.

The Treasure of Fisher's Cove. Tom Snyder Productions, 90 Sherman Street, Cambridge, MA 02140.

Wheel of Fortune. Sharedata, Inc., 7400 W. Detroit Street, Chandler, CA 85226.

Where in the World is Carmen Sandiego? Broderbund Software, 17 Paul Drive, San Rafael, CA 94903.

Index

About the Authors

Rena Soifer designed and implemented the Academy at Eastern Michigan University and has directed the program since she developed it in 1979. She is a Workplace Education Specialist with the Division of Corporate Services at Eastern Michigan University. She has an Education Specialist degree from Bowling Green State University, Ohio, and is a doctoral candidate at the University of Michigan. She was a high school reading and English teacher in Ohio. Both the Michigan Reading Association and the Michigan State Department of Education have given her awards for her role as an adult literacy educator.

Martha E. Irwin is Professor of Teacher Education at Eastern Michigan University, teaching courses in reading methods and computer applications in instruction. Her bachelor's and master's degrees are from Bowling Green State University, Ohio, and her Ed.D. is from Western Reserve University. She has experience as a classroom teacher and a curriculum consultant in Ohio. She is the co-author of *The Community Is the Classroom* and has published in *The Reading Teacher, Journal of Reading, Computers in the Schools, Journal of Reading Education,* and *Michigan Reading Journal.*

Barbara M. Crumrine has been with the Eastern Michigan University Academy since 1980 and is currently an assistant director of the project. Prior to joining the Academy, she was a classroom teacher in the Detroit metropolitan area. She received a bachelor's degree from Eastern Michigan University and has done graduate work at the University of Michigan and Michigan State University.

Emo Honzaki, currently an assistant director of the Eastern Michigan University Academy, has been with the project since 1979. She teaches classes in reading, writing, GED, business Japanese, and college study strategies. Her formal educational background includes a B.A. from the University of Chicago and an M. Ed. from Wayne State University, Detroit.

Blair K. Simmons teaches mathematics courses for the Eastern Michigan University Academy and recently directed a national industrial mathematics training project. As a former associate director of the Academy, she had major responsibility for assessment procedures. She has been an adult education teacher and a lecturer in the Department of Teacher Education at Eastern Michigan University, has an M.A. degree from Eastern Michigan University, and is pursuing a J.D. degree from Detroit College of Law.

Deborah L. Young is co-director of the Eastern Michigan University Academy. She has taught in public schools in Maine and Michigan. She is a lecturer in the Department of Teacher Education at Eastern Michigan University and a regional consultant for the national Adult Literacy and Technology Project. Her M.A. degree is from Eastern Michigan University and she is currently pursuing a doctoral degree at the University of Michigan. She has published in *Educational Technology, Journal of Reading*, and *Michigan Reading Journal*.